Contents

Introduction 4

6   House-Attached Patio Roofs
8   Freestanding Pergolas
10   Entryways
12   Gazebos
14   Garden Overheads
16   Arbor Benches
18   Garden Rooms
20   Entertaining Spaces

Planning & Design 22

22   Evaluating Your Needs
25   Design Basics
28   Selecting Materials
40   Working With Pros

Building Methods 44

44   Structural Anatomy
47   Buying Materials
52   Toolkit
55   Building Tips
58   Installing a Ledger
60   The Foundation
68   Posts & Beams
71   Installing Rafters
74   Roofing the Structure
76   Open-Style Roofing
78   Solid Roofing
80   Applying Asphalt Shingles
81   Applying Wood Shingles
82   How to Build a Gazebo
88   Finishing Wood Parts
89   Wiring an Outdoor Shelter

Step-By-Step Projects 92

92   Patio Shade Structure
96   Hillside Gazebo
101   Spa Shelter
106   Tea Arbor
111   Traditional Trellis
116   Open Shelter
120   Simple Square Structure
124   House-Attached Overhead
128   Corner Gazebo Bench
132   Open-Air Gazebo
138   Contemporary Trellis
144   Garden Retreat
148   Garden Bower
153   Garden Room Gazebo

Resources & Credits 158
Index 159

Introduction

We love outdoor living: lingering in the gardens we tend, entertaining our friends, enjoying a moment of solitude. While the combination of earth and elements is seductive on its own, often it is the man-made structures—simple arbors, classical pergolas, romantic gazebos, whimsical garden rooms, stately pavilions—that have the power to transform a front yard or backyard into something magical. Far from being merely decorative, outdoor structures have their practical sides, ranging from providing vertical and overhead plant support to creating additional square footage for living and dining space. By managing sun, wind, and weather, an addition that is as basic as a patio roof—open-raftered or closed, freestanding or attached to the house—not only improves the quality of backyard living but also extends the amount of time during the year one can comfortably spend outdoors. The more enticing the structure—a shady arbor bench or swing, an entertaining space heated by a wood-burning fireplace and furnished as comfortably as your living room—the more it increases the value of your property.

Adding structures to your yard starts with imagination, and that is where this book begins. The opening gallery section will get your creative juices flowing. The planning and design chapter will tell you everything you need to know about how to choose a site, select materials, and establish your budget. The building methods section takes the process a step further, showing you how to design and build a patio roof and put together a gazebo from a prefabricated kit. We end with more than a dozen plans for building a sampling of structures, from simple to challenging. In addition, at the end of every plan, there are sketchbooks that build on each project's theme to keep your flight of fancy going.

PATIO ROOFS & gazebos

Edited by Don Vandervort and the Editors of Sunset Books

Sunset Books • Menlo Park, California

Sunset Books

VICE PRESIDENT & GENERAL MANAGER: Richard A. Smeby
VICE PRESIDENT & EDITORIAL DIRECTOR: Bob Doyle
DIRECTOR OF OPERATIONS: Rosann Sutherland
MARKETING MANAGER: Linda Barker
ART DIRECTOR: Vasken Guiragossian
SPECIAL SALES: Brad Moses

Patio Roofs & Gazebos was produced
in conjunction with HomeTips, Inc.
EDITOR: Don Vandervort
MANAGING EDITOR: Louise Damberg
ASSISTANT EDITOR: Gabriel Vandervort
COPY EDITOR: Kristinha M. Anding
CONTRIBUTING EDITOR: Carol A. Crotta
GRAPHIC DESIGNER: Dan Nadeau
ILLUSTRATOR: Bill Oetinger

PREPRESS COORDINATOR: Eligio Hernandez
PRODUCTION SPECIALIST: Linda M. Bouchard
DIGITAL PRODUCTION: Mark Hawkins/Leisure Arts

COVER: Photography by Jamie Hadley
COVER LANDSCAPE DESIGN: Michael Glassman/
Michael Glassman & Associates
PHOTO STYLING: JoAnn Masaoka Van Atta

For additional copies of *Patio Roofs & Gazebos*
or any other Sunset book, visit us at
www.sunsetbooks.com or call (800) 526-5111.

This patio roof with attached gazebo extends the home's living space while seamlessly blending with the house's rustic architecture.

House-Attached Patio Roofs

Painted the same color as the wood siding, this patio roof establishes a harmonious transition from indoor space to outdoor living room.

Between house and yard there lies—with smart planning—a comfortable transitional space: the patio. The best patios are true extensions of the house in terms of comfort yet open to the pleasures of the outdoors. Undoubtedly, the most successful and useful patios are the ones that offer some measure of shelter from the sun and other weather elements. That is precisely where the patio roof comes into play.

A patio roof, like many other outdoor structures shown in these pages, can be constructed as

a freestanding entity. But, if your patio lies right out the back door and the rest of your yard does not have enough room to accommodate a separate structure, it only makes sense to attach at least one side of the patio roof to the house. The main reason to do so is that, if attached correctly, a patio roof receives the most solid support from a house's structure. Of course, there are other aesthetic and practical reasons. A house-attached roof establishes the patio as a true extension of the house—an outdoor room, as it were. It makes the transition from indoors to outdoors literally and visually seamless. Also, if your kitchen is at the back of the house, it makes outdoor entertaining simple. In addition, an attached patio roof provides shade not just for the patio but also for the back of the house, with the added benefit of lower energy bills in summer.

When designing an attached patio roof, there are some rules of thumb. While a patio can have its own personality, the roof structure should echo, not fight, the style of the house. First of all, the roof should be in scale

with the house; painting it the same color as the exterior woodwork so it blends in well is a simple solution. You will want to position it high enough to avoid a closed-in feeling, both from underneath the roof and inside the house, and set the spacing of the rafters to avoid cutting off too much light to the house's back windows.

Above: An inverted corner allows a roof to attach on two sides, providing filtered shade for several rooms.

A plain-Jane back porch becomes a lively pavilion with an elaborately rendered attached structure.

Freestanding Pergolas

The term "pergola" can be confusing to many. An Italian word, it means "arbor," an overhead plant support, but, in particular, it denotes a walkway formed by connected or unconnected arbors. That definition is a useful way of thinking about pergolas. Rather than a gazebo, which is a structure to sit inside and under, or an arbor, which sometimes features a bench on which to rest, a pergola encourages you to walk, to travel from point A to point B. As such, a pergola becomes a very useful, and beautiful, tool in both the front and back gardens. It directs traffic, if you will, in a stylish way, carrying inhabitants and guests on a sun-dappled path, often with flower- and vine-covered rafters lending sensual pleasures of sight and smell.

Pergolas, as connectors, can make an entryway statement as a pathway from curb to front door (see Entryways, pages 10–11). A short pergola can also make a smart transition from driveway or garage to yard. Pergolas work wonders, adding interesting structure to an otherwise bland yard. You can use a pergola to guide guests to back areas of the garden; to a pool or a spa; to a dining pavilion or a gazebo; or even, simply, to a secluded bench.

The most common styles used for pergolas are classical, with round columns, and Craftsman, with notched rafters, but there are many other designs from which to choose. Common plantings include climbing roses, wisteria, grapes, and other vining

Making the trip as interesting as the final destination, a pergola-lined path lends stateliness to a modest outdoor dining area, top, and provides a whirlwind walk through a lushly planted garden, right.

Left: A study in contrasts, this simply constructed pergola walkway uses meticulously clipped boxwood borders as a perfect foil for the rambling citrus branches overhead. Below: Pergolas make effective design tools to frame artfully constructed views.

plants, but just as often, pergolas are left bare so their architecture can be admired easily.

When planning a pergola, think of the effect you would like to achieve. Pergolas that curve can make a smaller yard seem bigger because they reveal the garden slowly through the spaces between the arbors. The structure of a straight pergola will frame what lies at its end, so plan and plant that space for maximum dramatic impact.

Entryways

s the principal entry to a house, the front door is meant to be welcoming, to be sure, but the front door does not necessarily need to be immediately revealed. In fact, as designers have long understood, creating a little anticipation in the journey from sidewalk to door can have its share of rewards. Attenuating the arrival at the entry, if properly done, not only adds visual interest and another layer of complexity to a property's overall impression, but it can also translate into real value through enhanced curb appeal. Interesting pathways and well-designed landscaping are the building blocks, and attached or freestanding pergolas, arbors, and other structures can help complete the look.

An entryway, like an hors d'oeuvre before the main meal, should enhance the experience, not detract from it. To that end, its design must take its cues from the home's architecture. Nothing looks more out of place than a gingerbready arbor in front of a stark modern house, or a stiffly geometric pergola in front of a country cottage. That said, there are plenty of houses that boast no definite style. For them, an interesting, and even bold, entryway structure can make a design statement, infusing the property with personality.

An attached structure should seem a natural extension of the house, using the same, or complementary, materials and style. There is a little more freedom with freestanding structures. In planning your entryway, you will want to make sure to not overwhelm the actual entry, or make the approach seem formidable. Overlandscaping can be a problem, particularly with a close succession of arbors or a long pergola. Planted with roses or vines, these structures can be inviting, but, if the plants are not properly maintained, they can become darkly overgrown and downright offputting. A little perspective goes a long way to creating an entryway that leaves visitors eager for more.

An easy roofline extension, supported by charming flared posts, adds depth to this plain clapboard home—without compromising the house's architectural simplicity.

Left: The starkness of this open-grid structure echoes the shape of the window banks behind it while defining the entry "space."

Below: This multi-columned colonnade, with its decorative rooftop railing, establishes formality and stateliness in a common clapboard two-story while at the same time creating an open-air porch.

Above: This freestanding arbor, rising out of fencing and banisters, sets the tone for the entry, which itself boasts a rafter-topped attached arbor.

Gazebos

A quiet conversation corner off the busy main deck, this gazebo blends perfectly with its surroundings while offering well-rounded views.

By far, the most popular freestanding garden structure today is the gazebo, and it is no wonder why. The first gazebos appeared in ancient Egyptian gardens some 5,000 years ago, and their popularity continued throughout ancient Rome and Greece, Persia, China, Japan, Renaissance Europe, and the American colonies. In the course of such a long and glorious history, these structures have taken many forms, but all gazebos share certain qualities. They are freestanding, rounded, or multisided (the octagonal shape is a more modern conceit), and open to some extent on all sides. They have a roof, usually in the form of a cupola. Most important, they are placed into the garden, when possible, on a height or spot with a beautiful view. A 360-degree view was key to the gazebo's nature—thus the derivation of its name, a shortening of the term "gaze about." As their many admirers know, gazebos provide the perfect spot to rest and take refuge while appreciating the beauty of nature.

Victorian gingerbread trim lends a bright touch to this octagonal gazebo.

Even on small lots, gazebos have their place. Generally constructed of wood, either painted or left to weather naturally, they can take on a number of styles, from simple to fancy. Some are left completely open, others are enclosed by banisters, and still others feature screened or glass windows and doors. Gazebos can be custom-made by professionals, built from scratch by intrepidly skilled homeowners, or assembled from the multitude of gazebo kits available.

In this modern age, gazebos know no bounds. Some house soaking pools or hot tubs, others are earmarked to be teahouses, conversation centers, meditation rooms, home offices, or dining pavilions. If your dreams for an outdoor structure take the shape of a gazebo, be sure to set it in a garden rather than against a wall or fence to ensure that every facet offers a blissful view, if only of a favored rose bush.

Above and left: Gazebos can be screened or left open, as these examples show, but they always are roofed.

Garden Overheads

I n Latin, the word "arbor" means tree. If you look back at some of the early uses of the word, you will see that a garden arbor is considered a treelike framework whose primary purpose is to support rambling, climbing, or vining plants in a way that creates a bower, or cocoon-like retreat. The notion that a person might need a haven from nature's vastness and wildness is an ancient one in our collective consciousness. Intertwined tree limbs, shrubs, and twining vines could naturally provide shelter, but people can also construct an arbor, cloaking it with plants of their choice.

In our suburban, lot-bound homes, we may no longer look at nature as something that needs to be tamed. Garden overheads, however, still have great appeal, and for many of the original reasons. They give structure to a yard, first of all, but they also define an open space to human scale, setting a boundary, however porous, between us and the sky. When used as plant supports, overheads can enclose us in a leafy and often flower-strewn bower that provides luxurious comfort.

Garden overheads can be used to great design effect in a yard. They can be the simplest of structures—comprising two posts and a crossbeam—or elaborate multilevel constructions. Overheads can establish a sitting area or patio space, extend the roofline of a house or garage, or mark way stations on a path through the garden. The amount of shelter they provide depends upon the spacing of rafters and the density of the plants that ramble across them. However they are used, remember that overheads create a ceiling, so the height of the posts supporting the overhead is critical—too short, and the space can feel claustrophobic, too tall, and their power to establish proportion is lost.

The simplest of overheads supports climbing plants up the sides and across the top, creating a human-scale doorway to the garden.

The blunt-cut rafters of this patio overhead reach out with open arms to visitors calling at the garden gate.

Below: Like a carefully planted grove of trees, these posts feature interconnected rafter "branches" that support rambling vines and visually enclose a dining area.

Left: An overhead's angularity is softened and its open spaces are filled in by leafy climbers, which shelter a bench.

Arbor Benches

The arbor bench is one of the simplest, yet most rewarding, of garden structures. Tucked in a cluster of green along a path or against a wall, a wood or metal arbor surrounding and supporting a bench or swing seems almost like a landscaping afterthought, but it may quickly become the most sought-after spot in the yard. Not as formal or social a space as a gazebo or garden room, not as transitory as a pergola, the arbor bench is a contemplative creature, intended to be a stopping place for one or maybe two. It offers the possibility of a private conversation, a good read, a nap, or simply a perch from which to admire the garden's splendor.

The beauty of the arbor bench is the adaptability of its design and its ability to find a place within almost everyone's budget. Most arbor benches are made of wood of some kind, from refined to rustic varieties. They can be dressed up with multiple layers of beams, rafters, and columns, as well as a variety of trims. Or, they can be pared down to four posts and crossbeams.

A rustic arbor bench is never more appealing than when it artfully blends into a bountifully planted garden.

Left and below: Securely attached swinging seats enhance the restful nature of these arbors.

Whether intended to stand out or blend in, they all offer an inviting seat, and that is the secret of their charm.

To landscape for an arbor bench, you will want to choose the surrounding plants strategically. Look for vining or climbing plants that do not drop excessive amounts of leaves—and do not drop fruit or berries at all, which can stain clothing and attract bees. If allergies are a problem, you may want to stay away from heavily scented flowers and high pollinators. If you like a great deal of shade, position the arbor bench in the coolest spot and establish thick-growing plants up and across the supports. If you prefer a sunnier place, train plants up the support posts but not across the top and space rafters to allow in the amount of sun you like.

While the typical arbor bench is built for one or two people, the more substantial the seating structure, the more social the area becomes.

Garden Rooms

With many homeowners today seeking to maximize the usefulness of their properties, the garden room has become a popular option where space permits. More completely constructed than a gazebo, but smaller than, say, a pool house or guesthouse, the garden room is something of a retreat. Generally, it will be watertight, with operable windows and a door. Because it is often weatherproof, a garden room can be used year-round and can host the same accoutrements as a comfortable room in the main house—upholstered furniture, rugs, computer equipment, lamps, heating and cooling systems, and storage components. Often it will include electrical systems and even running water. Some are outfitted with small kitchens, where building codes allow.

The advantages of a garden room are many. It can be an office for those who work at home or a sanctuary when the house is too congested. Older children can use it for homework or study, and it is particularly useful when children share bedrooms. Like a gazebo, it can be a

Above: A garden room becomes a year-round haven when enclosed with windows and doors.

Right: This clever vaulted-roof design gives the illusion of closure but is decidedly open-air.

Left and below: The garden room as al fresco living room: Furnishing the space as you would a room of your house brings all the comforts of home to the great outdoors.

quiet place for lunch or tea with a friend. Artists, knitters, and craftspeople can make a garden room the headquarters for their activities, with all their materials organized in one compact space. Done on a grander scale, the garden room can be a formal dining room or sitting room separate from the house.

When siting a garden room, the one major concern is that it receive proper natural light—enough so that you can see well and stay warm in the winter, but not so much as to overheat you in the summer. Landscaping can be helpful in this regard, and you may want to take advantage of natural overhead shelters—that is, trees—already in place. When done right, a garden room can become everyone's favorite space.

Entertaining Spaces

Proper spacing of overhead slats helps regulate sunshine while providing for ample air circulation—a key consideration when using the grill.

Entertaining outdoors is one of life's great pleasures and is made even greater when the patio or garden is properly prepared to host the event. Creating a comfortable space for entertaining, whether for casual conversation and drinks, al fresco dining, or even cooking the meal itself, requires structure. The best outdoor entertainment centers marry open-air breeziness with the warmth and comfort of an interior room. Partial walls, fireplaces, cooking islands, proper lighting, and furnishings all contribute their share to creating the sense of space, to be sure. Some type of overhead structure, however, is essential to corral the great outdoors into well-scaled intimacy.

Because many outdoor entertainment areas lie immediately outside the house proper, overhead structures frequently are attached to the house, a construction task that can take some expertise to avoid mistakes that could compromise the main house. The remaining supports usually are columns or posts set into the patio itself or into surrounding walls. Not all entertaining spaces are directly adjacent to the house, however. Freestanding dining pavilions, set on the far side of a pool or at the end of a well-lit meandering garden path, can be magical.

As you plan your entertaining space, you will first need to decide how much of the year you want to use it—and, naturally, this will depend on where you live. Areas subject to rain and colder weather may demand a solid roof structure and more enclosure. Sunbelt areas will benefit from slatted overheads that

provide shade as well as good air circulation. As for design, the look and materials of the entertaining space should seem a natural extension of the house yet evoke a personality all their own.

A solid roof structure, combined with a generously sized fireplace, allows for near year-round use of this cooking and dining center.

The charming mixture of shapes and materials, plus a formal fireplace set at an angle, gives this outdoor living room verve and personality.

Planning & Design

When it comes to building patio roofs, gazebos, or any other home improvement project, planning is the most important step in the process. Without planning, the likelihood of mistakes increases—and so does the time and money required to fix them.

Planning is even more important when you are building a structure that will be a major addition to your house or landscape. Because such a structure must resist the elements, fulfill certain functions, and blend in seamlessly with your home's design, you will need to first consider your site, climate, legal restrictions, cost, and more.

Evaluating Your Needs

As you look through the various shelters in this book, pay particular attention to the functions each serves. Then ask yourself which ones best meet your needs. Following are key priorities to consider:

In addition to creating a shady outdoor space, a patio roof reduces the sun's penetration of the home's interior.

A well-designed and carefully sited outdoor structure has the added benefit of increasing a home's living space.

Below: With a solid roof, this patio is transformed into a true outdoor room that is usable year-round.

Controlling sun exposure An overhead above a patio or deck can convert a sun-baked surface into a cool, inviting oasis. At the same time, it will cut down on glare and reduce the sun's penetration of your home's interior, resulting in lower energy bills during the warm summer months.

Shedding rain A solid roof shelters a deck or patio from rain, extending the period the outdoor area can be used. In addition, a solid patio roof can protect doorways and help direct rainwater away from the house. And outdoor furniture and equipment can be safely stored beneath it.

Extending livable space Patio roofs, pavilions, and garden entertainment structures can draw guests outside, taking the burden off your home's kitchen, dining, and living areas. When your outdoor rooms are equipped with barbecues, work surfaces, seating areas, and even fireplaces, they make entertaining a delight.

Adding visual interest A well-designed patio roof or deck overhead can dramatically improve your home's appearance, giving a nondescript roofline or facade new dimension. Poolside or in the garden, a pavilion or gazebo introduces a dynamic architectural element and creates a focal point in your landscape. A series of overheads can integrate several backyard features, such as a deck, pool, and dining area.

Increasing your home's value A new patio roof or gazebo, if well integrated and built with care, enhances not only your home's appearance but also its livability, both of which add to a house's resale value.

Enhancing privacy & comfort If your home is located in an area where houses are built close together, an outdoor shelter provides a measure of privacy and a feeling of cozy intimacy.

Clockwise from above: This stately pavilion adds a dramatic focal point to the backyard. Especially where quarters are tight, an outdoor structure can provide privacy and intimacy. A well-integrated overhead increases a home's practical and financial value.

Design Basics

An outdoor structure should harmonize with the architectural style of your home. While it is not essential that an overhead be built from the same materials as your house, the makeup of your new structure should complement your home.

An outdoor structure also should not block desired light or views. Beams that are too low will pull your viewable horizon down. Generally, the lowest beam should not be placed any less than 6 feet, 8 inches from the interior's finished floor surface.

An outdoor shelter should blend in with a home's style and surroundings.

Choosing a Site

For many overhead projects, the site is pre-determined by your needs. The deck requires shelter from the elements. The patio needs relief from the intense summer sun. The pool area would be enhanced by a spacious entertainment center.

If, on the other hand, you are rethinking your yard or developing a comprehensive landscaping plan, you will want to review a couple of basic site considerations:

Relationship to the house As you consider different locations for an overhead or gazebo, evaluate each area of your yard with respect to its accessibility to and from the house, any already-established traffic patterns, and the views you want to preserve or obscure.

Relationship to the yard Study your yard—its contours and views, the location of trees, and any other relevant elements—and

Both the gazebo, left, and pavilion, below, are sited to be destinations unto themselves.

try to maximize its assets. Also take note of its shortcomings, including drop-offs, areas that drain poorly or have unstable soil, and exposures to blazing sun or strong winds.

Microclimates

Sun, wind, and rain affect different parts of your property in different ways. In planning an outdoor structure, you will need to understand your yard's microclimate.

The sun's path In general, a patio that faces north is cool because the sun rarely shines on it. A south-facing patio is usually warm because, from sunrise to sunset, the sun never leaves it. Patios on the east side stay cool because they receive only morning sun, while west-facing areas can be uncomfortably hot because they absorb the full force of the sun's afternoon rays.

The sun crosses the sky in an arc that changes slightly every day, becoming lower in winter and higher in summer (see the illustration at left). In the dead of winter, the sun tracks across the sky at a low angle, throwing long shadows; on long summer days, it moves overhead at a very high angle. The farther north you live from the equator, the more extreme are the angles.

Rain & snow If you live in an area that experiences heavy snowfall and your proposed overhead has solid roofing, the structure must be able to handle the weight. In addition, you must carefully consider the effect of the structure's runoff from rain and snow.

When planning for a patio roof or gazebo, make sure to take into account its orientation to the sun.

SUMMER

AUTUMN & SPRING

WINTER

S

W

N

E

Legal Restrictions

First and foremost, contact your building department to learn about what regulations apply to outdoor structures in your area.

Building codes These set minimum safety standards for materials and construction techniques, such as the depth of footings; the size and type of posts, beams, and other structural members; and requirements for steel reinforcing in foundations.

Building permits Depending on a structure's size, whether or not it will be attached to the house, and its intended use, permits are often required. Projects entailing electrical or plumbing will almost certainly require permits for each.

Zoning ordinances Ordinances restrict the height of residential buildings, limit lot coverage (the amount of the lot a building or group of buildings may cover), specify setbacks (how close to the property lines a structure can be built), and, in some regions, stipulate architectural design standards.

Though overheads, gazebos, and other garden structures rarely exceed height limitations, they sometimes are affected by setback requirements. These structures also add to your overall lot coverage, an important consideration if you anticipate adding on to your home.

Drawing a Design

If you are planning a patio or deck overhead, a good scale drawing will show you how well the design will work with your house and how it will fit into the house-garden relationship. If you are planning a gazebo or other detached garden shelter, the drawing will enable you to visualize logical traffic patterns, as well as how the size and shape of the structure fits in with your home and yard.

Make a base map On graph paper, make a base map that shows the physical properties of your lot and house, including:

- Dimensions of your lot
- Siting of your house, as well as your pool and any other structures
- Doors and windows and their rooms
- Points of the compass showing how your house is situated
- Path and direction of the sun throughout the year and any hot spots
- Utilities (water, gas, and sewer lines) and the depth of each, as well as underground and overhead wires
- Setback lines
- Direction of prevailing winds
- Trees and other large plantings
- Any obstructions beyond the lot that affect sun, wind, views, or privacy

Experiment Using your base map, analyze the best location for your overhead or outdoor structure. Next, place tracing paper over the map and sketch your ideal design. Then, with a scale ruler, calculate what your structure's actual dimensions would be. Go out to the yard, and, using a tape measure, confirm its size and placement.

Before siting your structure, make a scale drawing of your house and yard to see how the addition will fit in.

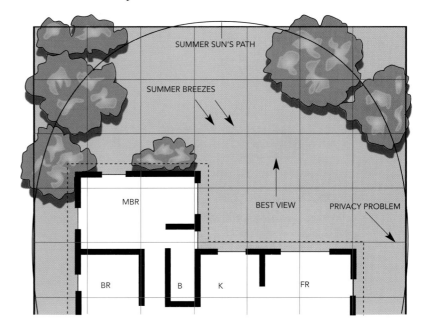

Selecting Materials

Most outdoor shelters are built from wood. Generally, the posts, beams, and rafters are made from dimension lumber; wood choices for roofs include boards, lath, battens, plywood, and woven wood.

Other popular roofing materials include outdoor fabrics, plastic or glass panels, and solid roofing such as wood or asphalt shingles. Posts can be made from concrete and stucco or steel instead of wood.

The following information will help you choose the appropriate materials for your project. For information on working with materials, turn to the Building Methods chapter, beginning on page 44.

Wood Basics

Wood is easy to cut, shape, and fabricate. It comes in a wide range of sizes, from thin lath to large beams, and in many species, grades, and textures. Wood's workability, variety, durability, and natural appearance make it an excellent choice for outdoor construction. For detailed information on choosing and buying lumber, as well as charts on dimensions and spans, see pages 47–49.

Because of its natural beauty and durability, wood is the most popular choice for outdoor structures.

Clockwise from left: Painting a structure often allows you to use a lesser grade of wood. Lodge poles are the perfect choice in this wooded setting. Vegas, Southwestern-style lodge poles, are the ideal complement to this house.

Lumber uses Thin lumber (less than ¾ inch thick) is commonly referred to as either lath or batten. The term "boards" generally denotes lumber that is ¾ or 1 inch thick and more than 2 inches wide. Lumber that is between 2 and 4 inches thick and is at least 2 inches wide is called dimension lumber. Timber is anything larger. Boards, dimension lumber, and timber are the most commonly used materials for posts, beams, rafters, and open-style roofing.

Another popular choice for open-style roofing is lath. Look for high-quality lath that does not have an excessive amount of knots or other defects. Relatively straight grain is also important to minimize the warping and twisting that the thin members can undergo with changing weather conditions.

Batten resembles overgrown lath; smooth-surfaced batten is sometimes called lattice, though the term "lattice" is also used to describe a crosshatch panel of lath material.

Lumber textures Milling can produce several different textures. Though surfaced lumber that is smooth is the most familiar, rough or resawn textures are available for a more rustic look.

Surfaced lumber, designated "S4S" ("surfaced on four sides"), is the standard for most construction. You can also buy lumber that has been planed on one, two, or three sides.

Rough lumber, which has been milled to size but not planed smooth, has a splintery

Steel, intentionally allowed to rust, provides a sturdy and stylish alternative to wood.

Plywood

In gazebo and patio roof construction, plywood occasionally serves as roof sheathing, aids in strengthening the structure, or assists in building concrete forms. Plywood siding occasionally covers gazebo walls or substitutes as a roofing material.

Standard plywood panels measure 4 by 8 feet, and their thicknesses range from $\frac{1}{4}$ to $\frac{3}{4}$ inch. Panels come in interior and exterior grades; choose the exterior grade where plywood will be exposed to the elements.

The appearance of a panel's face and back determines its grade, designated by the letters A through D (A being the highest and D the lowest). Exterior panels graded A/C are economical choices where only one side will be visible. Look for the grading on the face and back of the panels, as well as an association trademark that assures their quality.

Before using and after cutting plywood, seal all the edges with water repellent, stain

surface. Though buying rough lumber can save you money, pieces with excessive knots, flat grain, or high moisture content can warp and twist. Rough lumber can be stained, but it is a poor choice for painting.

Resawn lumber is wood that has been run through a coarse-bladed saw, such as a band saw, to create a scored texture. Though it is not stocked at most lumberyards, landscape professionals often special-order resawn lumber because of its rustic, but not too rough, texture and appearance. It can be very stable—though you will pay a premium for the best selection of boards—and it accepts wood stains easily and beautifully.

Sandblasted lumber is not a milled product, but it has a rustic appearance similar to resawn wood. Sandblasting surfaced lumber is generally not cost-effective unless you are having other sandblasting work done, on your siding or pool, for example.

Right: The use of tree stakes makes this overhead blend seamlessly into its surroundings.

sealer, or exterior house-paint primer to prevent moisture penetration (see "Finishing Wood Parts" on pages 88–90).

Other Wood Products

Though they do not fit into standard lumber categories, several other wood products are commonly used in the construction of outdoor overheads. Some are readily available; others require more searching or special-ordering. Many of them are chosen for their openness or to serve as an inexpensive support for flowering vines (see "Vines for Patio Roofs & Gazebos" on page 152).

Grape stakes Favorites of fence builders, these are easy to find at home and garden centers and lumber supply outlets and offer a hand-hewn look perfect for rustic, open-style roofing. Made from redwood or cedar, they are roughly 2 by 2 inches and come in 6-foot lengths. Split grape stakes, more the size of 1 by 2s, also make good overheads.

Poles Bean poles, 1-by-1-inch lengths of redwood or cedar, and preservative-treated lodge poles, vegas (Southwestern-style lodge poles), and tree stakes lend a very rustic appearance to an overhead. They are usually sold by specialty landscape supply companies and may have to be special-ordered.

Woven reed Readily available at many nurseries and garden supply centers, woven reed comes in 15- and 25-foot rolls that are 6 feet wide. For durability, the reed is woven with stainless-steel wire, which can be cut easily and retwisted after the roll is trimmed to the dimensions of the overhead. Because constant flexing of the wire strands causes them to fail quickly, nail or staple the material to a rigid frame. Be aware that woven reed will eventually rot with exposure to rain, but its affordability allows for replacement every two to three years.

Woven bamboo Manufactured primarily for shades, woven bamboo comes in rolls 3 to 12 feet wide and usually 6 feet long. Available in wired form, similar to reed, there are two main grades: split and matchstick. Split bamboo is much coarser and less regular than matchstick, which is made from thin strips of the inner layer of the bamboo stalk. The split type is preferable for most installations because it is stiffer; however, matchstick is better for an adjustable overhead because of its flexibility.

Woven spruce & basswood Similar to woven bamboo, these woods are generally woven with string, but a high grade of seine twine is employed for outdoor use.

A range of pole sizes gives this overhead a rustic appearance and sheds dramatic light.

Preassembled lattice panels lend a charming appearance and are an enormous time and labor saver.

Classical Greek-style columns create a stately look and the sturdiest of structures.

Preassembled lattice panels These panels offer the look of crisscrossed lath without the labor of measuring, cutting, and fastening each piece.

Wood lattice panels generally are manufactured in 4-by-8-foot; 2-by-8-foot; and, less commonly, 4-by-6-foot sizes. Several grades are available, but only redwood and cedar panels are durable enough for outdoor use. Patterns include diagonal and checkerboard designs, as well as variations on these themes.

Also available are vinyl lattice panels, which resemble finely painted wood lattice,

are smooth and very tough, and never need refinishing. They are more expensive than wood. Vinyl lattice panels are available in white and several earth tones and typically come in 4-by-8-foot or 2-foot, 10-inch-by-8-foot sizes.

Posts & Columns

Though wood posts are standard for most patio roofs and gazebos, concrete, steel, and other materials are sometimes used for particular reasons—to provide added strength or to blend with the style of the house, for example. For more about post materials and designs, see pages 68–71.

Architectural Classical and decorative columns are available through millwork dealers. Structural types are made from wood, aluminum, and fiberglass composites. Nonstructural types, usually designed to conceal a wood or steel post, are also made from these materials or from polyurethane. Many types of columns are sold as kits and may be enhanced by various decorative caps and bases.

Solid Roofing

If you are planning a solid-roof overhead or gazebo, you will want to consider its roof pitch, or slope, and your house's roof before deciding on a material.

Asphalt shingles Asphalt shingles, by far the most common solid roofing material, are economical, easy to install and maintain, and available in a broad range of colors, shapes, and patterns. They usually measure 12 by 36 inches.

Wood shingles Typically made from Western red cedar, wood shingles offer natural beauty and durability. They are, however, prohibited in some regions of the country because of their flammability, so check first with your local building department. Wood shingles are available in 16-, 18-, and 24-inch lengths.

Wood sidings Sidings are not meant to be watertight, finished-roofing materials,

Concrete & stucco Square or rectangular concrete columns are made by pouring concrete into wood forms. Cylindrical fiber tubes are used to form round columns. Stucco columns are constructed from concrete blocks or wood frames with plywood panels that are then stuccoed.

Steel Because structural steel is costly, it is often reserved for use where extreme loads must be carried over unstable soil. Impervious to fire, rot, and termites, steel posts offer exceptional endurance. Often, steel posts are hidden under a facade of wood. Steel structures must be professionally engineered and fabricated.

Top left: Square columns are most often made by applying stucco over plywood and wood framing. Bottom left: Decorative columns may be sold as kits and enhanced by various caps and bases.

Below: Because of their ability to conform to different profiles, wood shingles are excellent for curved roofs.

Solid roofing materials—such as (clockwise from above) tile, plywood, and copper—create the look of a more substantial structure and lend the ability to make a style statement.

but they can be serviceable for gazebos and similar structures if the roof is pitched for efficient water runoff. You will need to apply roofing felt underneath for rain protection and treat the siding with a sealant to withstand the elements.

The most appropriate patterns of solid-board siding for roofing are horizontal shiplap or bevel patterns that shed rain like shingles do. Redwood and cedar are the most popular species because of their natural resistance to decay. Boards are ¾ inch thick. Widths vary from 4 to 12 inches, and lengths run up to 20 feet.

Plywood sidings can also serve as roofing. They come in sheets, which allow you to cover a large surface quickly, or in lapboards. The standard sheet size is 4 by 8 feet. Lapboards are 6 to 12 inches wide and 16 feet long. Unfinished varieties must be treated with a durable finish.

Other solid roofing materials Nearly any solid roofing material that is used on a house, from concrete tile to metal, can be applied to a patio roof or gazebo. These materials, however, generally require that installation be done by a professional.

Plastic & Glass Roofing

Plastic or glass can be ideal roofing choices when you want protection from the elements but maximum exposure to sunlight and starry skies.

Acrylic plastic Because it resists shattering, weighs less than glass, and comes in transparent or translucent varieties, acrylic is a practical choice for many structures. In addition, sheets of acrylic are easy to cut, shape, drill, and fasten with only fairly standard woodworking tools.

On the downside, acrylic scratches easily. For this reason, you may want to limit its use to a site away from trees or in areas of the

structure where scratches will go unnoticed.

Acrylic plastic also comes opaque and in almost every color of the rainbow, but remember that colored plastic will shed the same color light.

Thicknesses range from ⅛ to ½ inch, and, of course, the thicker the material, the more expensive it is. But a thicker panel will require less support to prevent it from sagging, and it will be less likely to crack.

To find acrylic-plastic dealers, look under "Plastics—Rods, Tubes, Sheets, Etc." in the

Asphalt roofing shingles are economical and long-lasting; the glass at the roof's crown allows in light and creates visual interest.

Acrylic plastic is durable as well as ideal for letting in sunlight, particularly for structures in shady, cool areas.

telephone directory or search the Internet for "acrylic plastic sheets" in your area.

Polyester resin & vinyl Commonly referred to as "fiberglass," these widely used materials are, in fact, often plastic that is reinforced with fiberglass for added strength. Translucent types are the most popular and come in several patterns: corrugated, flat, crimped, staggered shiplap, and simulated board-and-batten. Opaque corrugated vinyl panels, designed to block light entirely, are also available.

Standard panel sizes range from 24 to 50½ inches in width and from 8 to 20 feet in length. Thickness varies by color and type. Corrugated rolls run 40 inches wide; flat rolls run 36 inches wide.

Glass Because glass is relatively expensive, quite heavy, fragile, and very tricky to work with, it is best to consult a professional if you want to use it. Also be advised that in nearly all overhead applications, building codes closely regulate the acceptable types of glass and supporting framework.

Outdoor Fabrics

Canvas and similar fabrics are favored by many for awnings and patio roofs. These fabrics can block or diffuse sun, shed rain, and add a touch of color and texture. They can draw taut into flat planes, curve gracefully over vaulted frames, or hang and then gather like curtains.

Because these fabrics are lightweight, the supporting structure can often be lightweight, as well (though windy regions may require engineered framing). Many installations also offer removable fabric.

The specialty fabrics discussed on the following pages can be found and custom-sewn at awning dealers. Look through samples for colors, patterns, and properties that are right for your application.

Cotton duck Popularly known as canvas, cotton duck comes in a variety of solid colors and in stripes. The painted type has a coat of acrylic paint on its weather-facing surface, which makes the duck opaque. But because the paint has a dull finish, it leaves the linen texture visible; from the underside, the surface appears pearl green. Painted duck will eventually become brittle over time, but with normal maintenance it should last five to eight years.

Dyed duck has color that runs throughout the fabric. It can be waterproofed to extend its life, but generally it will not last as long as painted duck. Also, because the fabric is uncoated, it is more prone to mildew.

Acrylic fabric Though acrylic fabric is priced competitively to canvas, it is nearly twice as durable. In addition, it sheds rain without leaking.

The man-made fiber, which lasts five to 10 years, has a soft, woven look and comes in a broad palette and many patterns. Acrylic fabric is generally translucent, though the degree of opacity varies with the color. Because the fabric is woven, it is also colorfast; however, colors may not be as crisp as painted-on hues.

Under normal conditions, acrylic will not mildew, unless leaves and debris are left to rot on top of it. Occasional hosing accompanied by a light brushing to remove dirt and debris will not only help to prolong the fabric's life but also maintain its beautiful appearance.

The weight of acrylic fabric is typically 8½ ounces per square yard. The width is normally 46 inches, though 60-inch widths are available in some marine grades.

Vinyl-coated cotton canvas The shiny weather-facing surface of this fabric shows little or no texture; its underside is

The various types of outdoor fabrics provide an inexpensive alternative to solid or open roofing and, depending on the type chosen, can let in partial light or no light at all.

Outdoor fabric designed to fit a frame is a convenient installation. In some cases, this type of "roofing" can simply be removed during winter and the rainy seasons.

Right: The addition of screening to an outdoor room is an ideal solution for regions where insects can present a real problem.

opaque and green-colored. Available in solid colors or in stripes (usually white with a primary color), it weathers and cleans well. Its life span is four to seven years.

Vinyl-laminated polyester

This fabric sandwiches an open-weave polyester scrim between two layers of painted vinyl. The scrim allows light to pass through, making the area below brighter and warmer than with a solid fabric. Sold in a wide range of solid colors and stripes, vinyl-laminated polyester has a matte surface and an underside that may be either colored or sand white. This is a good choice for humid areas because it resists mildew. The material should last five to eight years, but the scrim can delaminate if it is folded repeatedly.

Screening Materials

Screening filters sunlight and, if the mesh is fine, prevents insects from entering. A wide array of screening materials is available; the most popular are made from aluminum or fiberglass woven in a mesh of 18 by 16 strands per square inch.

Hardware and home improvement stores stock some types. For other varieties, check

your telephone directory under "Screens—Door & Window," or search the Internet for door and window screens in your area.

Aluminum Corrosion-resistant aluminum screening has a long life expectancy in most parts of the country. But, as with other metals, it will deteriorate in coastal regions. If struck or strained, it tends to bulge rather than break.

Aluminum screening comes in three colors: black, dark gray, and bright aluminum. The darker the color, the better the visibility from inside. It is sold in rolls that are 7 or 25 feet long and 24, 28, 30, 32, 36, or 48 inches wide. (Rolls that are 100 feet long may be special-ordered in several widths, from 18 to 72 inches.)

Fiberglass Both strong and lightweight, vinyl-coated fiberglass is the most popular screening material. It does not corrode, rust,

oxidize, or stain, but it tears more easily than aluminum and may stretch. Strands of .013 millimeter are recommended for such outdoor enclosures as patio rooms and gazebos. Colors include silver, light and dark gray, and aquamarine. Fiberglass screening comes in the same lengths as aluminum and in widths up to 84 inches.

Porch screening Used for patio, porch, and gazebo enclosures (in addition to conventional window and door screens), tightly woven, vinyl-coated fiberglass solar, or "sun," screening dramatically blocks heat gain by reducing light transmission by 30 percent. It utilizes slightly larger, stronger strands than regular fiberglass screening and comes in a standard mesh size of 18 by 14; in areas where insects are abundant, 20-by-20 mesh is also available. Keep in mind, however, that the smaller the mesh, the more light and breezes will be cut down.

During the daytime, solar screen appears almost opaque from outside but offers good visibility from inside. It comes in five colors: charcoal and silver gray, the most commonly available; bronze; dark bronze; and gold.

Plastic mesh Because it is unaffected by humidity and salty air, plastic mesh is one of the best screening materials for use in coastal areas. Available by the running foot in widths of 24, 30, 36, 42, 48, and 72 inches, plastic mesh can be purchased by the roll or by the piece. Be aware that the wider it is, the more difficult it may be to pull tight and nail so the more likely it will be to sag.

Aluminum & plastic The horizontal wires of this screening hybrid—aluminum coated with plastic—are broad and flat to reduce sun penetration. A neutral gray, the screen is easy to see through from the inside yet appears opaque from outside, affording a measure of privacy.

Manufactured Structures

A popular option for homeowners who want a low-maintenance, easy-to-assemble patio roof or trellis is a manufactured metal system. Though some simple models of these may be constructed by experienced do-it-yourselfers, most types are intended to be assembled by factory-accredited fabricators.

Aluminum is the material of choice for residential units because it is lighter in weight, more affordable, and easier to tool compared with steel. Steel is used for commercial structures (such as those in parks) that are occasionally adapted for residential use. Both materials are given a durable powder-coated wood-toned or colored finish with a long-term warranty.

Although these structures look from a distance like they are made of wood, closer inspection reveals their stamped metal texture. This less-than-natural appearance is the trade-off for easy maintenance.

Working with Pros

Many homeowners who add an overhead or outdoor structure seek professional services, whether during the design or the construction phase. It pays to call a professional if a project will require engineering, complex components, hard-to-work-with materials, difficult siting, or other aspects that may push designing or building the structure beyond your skill set.

To find the appropriate professionals, ask friends or neighbors who have had similar work done. Trade associations also can recommend licensed professionals in your area, or you can check out Web sites that offer free referrals of pre-approved local professionals.

Structures that have special engineering needs and materials are best left to building professionals.

Design & Building Professionals

Following is a listing of some professionals whose services you may require, along with information about working with them:

Architects & landscape architects

These state-licensed professionals have degrees in architecture or landscape architecture. They are trained to create designs that are structurally sound and functional, as well

as aesthetically pleasing. They also know about construction materials and can purchase them, negotiate bids from contractors, and supervise the work.

Landscape & building designers

Though neither is licensed, landscape designers usually have a landscape architect's education and training. Building designers can offer construction help along with design work.

Draftspersons

Usually much less expensive than landscape architects or designers, a draftsperson can create working drawings, necessary to secure building permits, from which you or your contractor can work. Some also may provide designs. If you are adapting a plan in this book, a qualified draftsperson may be all you need.

Soils & structural engineers

You should consult specialists before building a structure on an unstable or steep lot or where there are considerable winds or loads. A soils engineer evaluates soil conditions at a proposed construction site and establishes design specifications for foundations that can resist the stresses unstable soil exerts. Structural engineers, often working with the calculations of a soils engineer, design foundation piers and footings to suit the site. They also may provide the wind- and load-stress calculations required.

General & landscape contractors

These professionals specialize in construction, though some also have design skills and experience. Contractors may do all the work or hire qualified subcontractors. They can order construction materials and ensure that the job is completed according to contract.

Subcontractors

Contractors who specialize in particular areas of construction—

For large or intricate structures, it is usually advisable to hire skilled professionals.

electrical, masonry, plumbing, and so forth—are known as subcontractors. If you act as your own general contractor, you will be responsible for hiring and supervising subcontractors, purchasing construction materials, and obtaining permits. When dealing with subcontractors, give them clear instructions, put all work requirements in writing, and provide as much direct supervision as possible.

The Process

Three common working arrangements are open to you if you choose to work with a designer or contractor:

Consultation

An architect or a landscape architect can review your plans, suggest ideas for a more effective design, and provide anything from a couple of rough conceptual sketches to complete drawings, working on an hourly basis or for a day rate.

Professional gazebo builders offer stock designs that they can then customize to a homeowner's specifications.

Fee Another route is to negotiate a flat fee for a given amount of work—for example, to design or modify your project and provide working drawings, with the understanding that you will oversee construction.

Planning through construction Last, you can retain designers or contractors on a planning-through-construction basis. In addition to designing your project, the professional will supervise or actually perform the project's construction.

Whichever option you choose, you do not necessarily want to choose the professional who gives you the lowest bid—and you want to solicit at least three bids. Also base your

When hiring a professional for an intricate structure such as a gazebo, make attention to detail a high priority.

decision on the individual's reputation, checking references carefully and asking to see some finished projects. The person should be well-established, cooperative, competent, and financially solvent. And, most important, the individual you choose should be someone with whom you feel comfortable personally and professionally.

Writing a Contract

If you decide to hire a contractor to build your outdoor structure, you will need to have a written contract. The more complete the contract, the better your chances that neither the process nor the result will be flawed. It is a good idea to consult a lawyer before signing any agreement for work on your property.

Here are the basic items that should be in any contract:

Construction materials All major materials, including hardware, should be identified by quality markings (species, grades, and other quality identifiers) and model numbers where applicable. Anything not included and added later will increase your costs.

Work to be performed For example, if you want the contractor to prepare the site, the contract should explicitly identify the tasks: removal of fences and shrubs, tearing out of concrete, grading, and so forth.

Time schedule This should include the beginning date, completion date, and ideally interim dates for completion of certain aspects of the job.

Method of payment It is standard practice for a small down payment to be made before work commences, for additional installments to be made at interim completion dates, and for the balance to be paid when all the work is completed.

Building a Budget

As with most construction projects, the two main factors determining cost are materials and labor.

Start by selecting your preferred materials (see the section on lumber on pages 47–49 to determine how many building units you will need), and then make changes or adjustments as your budget dictates. But do not cut costs by resorting to lower-quality materials. Instead, consider downsizing the dimensions of your structure, or substitute with equally durable but less costly materials (an asphalt-shingle roof instead of a wood-shingle roof, for example).

Of course, you can usually save considerably by doing the work yourself. But, even if you have the skills and experience to build your project, keep in mind the value of your time. A professional working with a helper or subcontractors might be able to accomplish in a few days what would take you weeks and possibly time away from your job. Also take inventory of your tool kit. If your project requires you to rent or buy several tools, it might be more cost-effective to contract out certain aspects.

Finally, do not forget to add in all fees for special services and permits. If your site requires consultation with a soils engineer, for example, you will need to add that to your budget. If your project includes plumbing or electrical, requiring the services of those professionals, you will not only incur those labor costs but most often the costs of permits for that work, as well.

If, after crunching the numbers, you still cannot bring your budget in where you need it to be, consider other options. You can choose a lesser grade of lumber, but keep in mind that your structure will have to be painted and then repainted every few years. Be sure to select boards that are straight and relatively free of knots so as not to compromise the integrity of the structure.

Or, consider siting your gazebo where the ground will not require as much grading or having your patio or deck overhead cover only a dining area. You can also save on costs by investigating gazebo kits or pre-manufactured shade structures, which, if you are not planning to do the work yourself, can add up to significant cost savings.

If you are buillding a complex structure on a tricky site, don't forget to budget for permits and special services.

Building Methods

I f building an outdoor structure sounds a bit intimidating, you will be happy to know that many of the designs featured in this book are relatively simple, requiring skills and tools that fall within the repertoire of most handy homeowners. These designs often employ a systems approach, with components that you build repeatedly to complete the structure.

It is a good idea to explore the following pages before finalizing your design or starting to build. Doing so will give you an overview of the project and help you gain a clear understanding of specifications in order to determine beam sizes, post spacing, and other important building details.

Most patio roofs and gazebos are made from components that you replicate and then piece together.

Structural Anatomy

As you can tell by paging through this book's ideas and projects, patio roofs and gazebos are as varied as their creators. Diminutive, bold, contemporary, classic, solid, airy—the options are endless. With this in mind, it can be a little tricky to discuss building methods because so many different techniques may be used during construction. In this chapter, we focus on the most common methods.

Most patio roofs and gazebos utilize the same basic components: foundation, posts or walls, beams, rafters (or joists), and some type of roofing. The typical construction of patio roofs and gazebos is shown on the following two pages.

Gazebos

Some gazebos sit on concrete slabs or patios; others have built-up floors that rest on a series of footings. Each type has its advantages. A concrete slab can be formed and cast in a day for a relatively low cost, particularly if you provide the labor. But casting concrete (see pages 64–67) can be a challenge for inexperienced do-it-yourselfers. A built-up floor is more attractive than a slab but can require exacting carpentry skills. A built-up floor also sits a little higher above the ground than a slab.

A gazebo's posts are fastened to the foundation or a sill of treated 2-by lumber with post anchors. The tops of the posts are secured to the beams by metal hangers or post caps; alternatively, you can toenail through the beams into the posts. Knee braces ensure a more rigid structure. The rafters radiate outward from a central hub and are joined to the top ends of the posts or to the beams. The gazebo may be capped with either solid or open roofing.

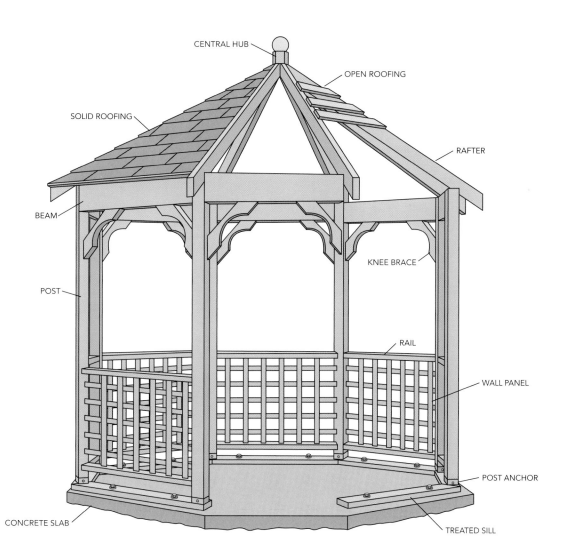

CENTRAL HUB

OPEN ROOFING

SOLID ROOFING

RAFTER

BEAM

KNEE BRACE

POST

RAIL

WALL PANEL

POST ANCHOR

CONCRETE SLAB

TREATED SILL

House-Attached

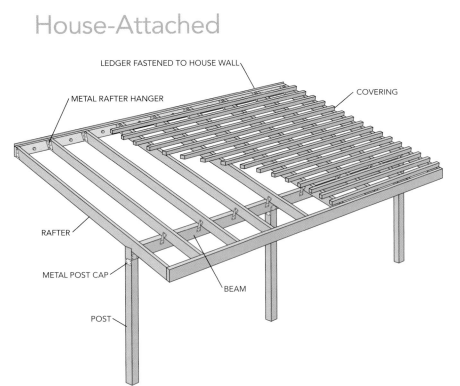

LEDGER FASTENED TO HOUSE WALL

METAL RAFTER HANGER

COVERING

RAFTER

METAL POST CAP

BEAM

POST

Patio Roofs

A patio roof or an overhead may be freestanding, such as the one shown below, or it can be attached to the house with a ledger, as shown at left. In either case, the structure is supported by a series of posts or columns, which in turn rest on a concrete slab or on piers and footings.

If you're adding an overhead to an existing deck, you can bolt the posts to the substructure of the deck, placing them directly above or adjacent to the deck posts. The posts support beams and rafters. If the overhead is attached to the house, the ledger takes the place of a beam, supporting the rafters directly. Overhead rafters can be left open or can be covered with any one of a number of materials, as discussed on pages 74–75.

Freestanding

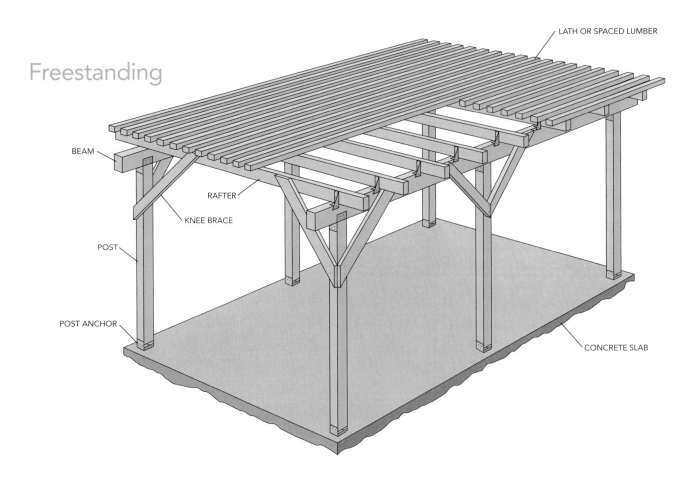

LATH OR SPACED LUMBER

BEAM

RAFTER

KNEE BRACE

POST

POST ANCHOR

CONCRETE SLAB

Buying Materials

Shopping for lumber, fasteners, and other materials can be daunting. If the choices don't overwhelm you, some of the prices probably will. The best way to get through the lumberyard or home improvement center with a minimum of confusion and expense is to go prepared. Know what to look for—types, sizes, and grades—and how materials are sold. The following primer can help you accomplish this.

When choosing materials, become familiar with the information beginning on page 28 regarding lumber and other materials.

When choosing materials, become familiar with the information beginning on page 28 regarding lumber and other materials.

From left to right: Pressure-treated Douglas fir, redwood, and Western red cedar are favorite choices for many outdoor structures.

Lumber

Regardless of the material you choose for the roof surface of your outdoor structure or overhead, its framework will most likely be constructed from wood. Following are some basic lumber-buying details.

Species Woods from different species of trees have varying properties. Redwood, cedar, and cypress heartwoods (the darker part of the wood, cut from the tree's core) have a natural resistance to decay. This characteristic, combined with the natural beauty of these woods, makes them a favorite for decking, natural-finish lath-type roofing, and similar applications. But these woods are usually more expensive than ordinary framing lumber such as Douglas fir, yellow Southern pine, and Western larch. So landscape professionals often specify framing lumber or preservative-treated woods for the structural parts of an overhead and save premium woods for where beauty is important.

Lumber is divided into softwoods and hardwoods, terms that refer to the origin of the wood, not its hardness (though most hardwoods tend to be harder than softwoods). Softwoods come from conifers; hardwoods come from deciduous trees.

As a rule, softwoods are much less expensive, easier to tool, and more readily available than hardwoods, so softwoods are chosen for nearly all outdoor construction projects.

Lumber grades At the mill, lumber is sorted and identified by name and, in many cases, by the species and grading agency.

Generally, lumber grades are determined by a number of different factors, including natural growth characteristics or blemishes such as knots; defects caused by milling errors; and techniques used for drying and preserving wood that affect strength, durability, or appearance.

Linear Feet vs. Board Feet

Lumber is sold either by the linear or board foot. The linear foot, commonly used for small orders, considers only the length of a piece. For example, 20 2 by 4s, 8 feet long, would be the same as 160 linear feet of 2 by 4.

The board foot is a common unit of measure for volume orders, and lumberyards often quote prices per 1,000 board feet. A piece of wood 1 inch thick, 12 inches wide, and 12 inches long equals 1 board foot. To compute board feet, multiply the thickness in inches by the width in feet by the length in feet. For example, a 1-by-6 board 10 feet long would be computed: 1 inch x ½ foot (6 inches) x 10 feet = 5 board feet.

When ordering lumber, however, you still must list the exact dimensions you need so your order can be filled correctly.

Grade-stamping by the American Wood Preserver's Bureau on pressure-treated lumber indicates the wood's appropriate usage.

When it comes to lumber grades, you get what you pay for. In most cases, higher grades cost far more than lower grades. The fewer the knots and other defects, the pricier a board will be. To save money on a project, pinpoint the lowest grade that will be suitable for each component.

Structural lumber and timbers are rated for strength. The most common grading system includes the grades Select Structural, No. 1, No. 2, and No. 3. For premium strength, choose Select Structural. Many lumberyards sell a mix of grades called No. 2-and-Better. Other grading systems used for some lumber classify wood according to the grades Construction, Standard, and Utility, or as a mixture of grades called Standard-or-Better.

Redwood is usually graded according to appearance and percentage of heartwood. Clear All heart is the best and the most expensive. B heart, Construction heart, and Merchantable heart are, in descending order of quality, typical grades of pure heartwood.

Cedar grades, starting with the highest quality, are Architect Clear, Custom Clear, Architect Knotty, and Custom Knotty, but these designations do not indicate whether or not the wood is heartwood.

Dimensions of Softwood Lumber

NOMINAL	ACTUAL (SURFACED)
1x2	¾" x 1½"
1x3	¾" x 2½"
1x4	¾" x 3½"
1x6	¾" x 5½"
1x8	¾" x 7¼"
1x10	¾" x 9¼"
1x12	¾" x 11¼"
2x2	1½" x 1½"
2x3	1½" x 2½"
2x4	1½" x 3½"
2x6	1½" x 5½"
2x8	1½" x 7¼"
2x10	1½" x 9¼"
2x12	1½" x 11¼"
4x4	3½" x 3½"
4x6	3½" x 5½"
4x8	3½" x 7¼"
4x10	3½" x 9¼"
6x8	5½" x 7¼"

Maximum Rafter & Beam Spans

An essential part of planning your project is determining the number, size, and spacing of rafters, beams, and posts, according to the loads they will carry.

In areas with mild climates, patio roofs are generally designed for loads of 30 psf (pounds per square foot). For heavy roofs or in areas with substantial snowfall or winds, call your local building department for code requirements.

The tables on the opposite page give maximum spans for rafters and beams. The figures are based on quality materials. For lesser grades, spans should be shorter. Keep in mind that these are maximums—in other words, shortening spans slightly will result in a more solid structure.

Find out the loads your overhead must bear, and then determine the rafter sizes. Next, calculate beam placements and how best to coordinate them with the rafters.

Treated lumber Though redwood and cedar heartwoods are naturally resistant to decay and termites, most other woods soon rot and weaken when in prolonged contact with soil or water. Common lumber such as Southern pine and Western hem-fir can be factory treated with chemical preservatives that guard against rot, insects, and other sources of decay. Termed "pressure-treated," this lumber is less expensive than redwood or cedar and, in some regions, more readily available. It can be used for structural members such as posts, beams, and rafters.

Pressure-treated wood is available in two "exposures." If it will be close to or touching the ground, the Ground Contact type is required. The Above Ground type is for other applications. The American Wood Preserver's Bureau, which governs the treatment industry, grade-stamps preservative-treated lumber according to each type's appropriate uses.

Treated lumber does have drawbacks. Unlike redwood and cedar, which are soft and therefore easy to cut and drive fasteners into, treated wood can be hard, brittle, and prone to warp and twist. Moreover, some people object to the greenish color of certain pressure-treated materials (though applying paint or a semitransparent stain can mask this) and the staple-like incisions that cover the surfaces of most types.

The primary preservative used for pressure-treated lumber contains chromium, a toxic metal. Wear safety glasses and a dust mask when cutting this type of lumber and wear gloves when handling it for prolonged periods. Never burn scraps of treated lumber.

Standard lumber sizes Lumber is normally stocked in lengths from 6 to 20 feet and in a broad range of widths and thicknesses. Different names are given to various size categories: boards, dimension lumber, lath, and so forth. For more about some of these, go to pages 28–30. Do note that the actual sizes of surfaced boards and dimension lumber are smaller than those suggested by their names, as shown in the chart on the opposite page. The difference is the amount reduced by shrinkage during drying and removed by planing.

To figure the minimum sizes for supporting loads, consult the charts below. Keep in mind that these are minimums for the spacing indicated—you can select larger sizes to handle excessive loads or for appearance. Of course, beefier sizes also increase your lumber bill.

From left to right, this redwood varies in grade from rough and knotty to clear. The higher the grade, the more attractive and decay-resistant the wood.

Maximum Rafter Spans

RAFTER SIZE	RAFTER SPACING		
	12"	16"	24"
2 by 4	9' 0"	8' 3"	7' 3"
2 by 6	14' 6"	13' 0"	11' 6"
2 by 8	19' 0"	17' 0"	15' 0"

Maximum Beam Spans

BEAM SIZE	SPACING BETWEEN BEAMS (OR BEAM TO LEDGER)				
	4 feet	8 feet	10 feet	12 feet	16 feet
2 by 6	7' 11"	7' 0"	6' 6"	6' 3"	5' 6"
2 by 8	10' 6"	9' 6"	8' 6"	8' 0"	7' 6"
2 by 10	13' 4"	12' 0"	11' 3"	10' 6"	9' 6"
2 by 12	16' 3"	14' 6"	13' 6"	12' 9"	11' 6"
4 by 4	6' 11"	6' 0"	5' 6"	5' 3"	4' 9"
4 by 6	10' 10"	9' 6"	8' 9"	8' 3"	7' 6"
4 by 8	14' 4"	12' 6"	11' 6"	11' 0"	10' 0"
4 by 10	18' 3"	16' 0"	14' 6"	14' 0"	12' 6"
4 by 12	22' 2"	19' 6"	18' 3"	17' 0"	15' 6"

Fasteners

Nails, bolts, screws, and metal connectors are used to link building materials and strengthen the areas they join. The following information will guide you in choosing appropriate fasteners.

Nails Nails are sold in 1-, 5-, and 50-pound boxes, as well as loose in bins. For outdoor use, choose hot-dipped galvanized, aluminum, or stainless-steel nails; other types will rust. In fact, even the best hot-dipped galvanized nail will rust over time, particularly at the exposed nailhead, which becomes battered by hammering. Stainless-steel or aluminum nails won't rust, but they are far more expensive than galvanized nails, and aluminum nails bend easily.

You will also need to choose between common and finishing nails. The common nail is favored for construction because it has an extra-thick shank and a broad head that grips the wood well. But where you don't want a nail's head to show, choose a finishing nail, which has a very small head. After you drive the slightly rounded head nearly flush, sink it below the wood's surface with a nailset.

Nail Equivalents

PENNY	ACTUAL
2d	1"
4d	1½"
6d	2"
8d	2½"
10d	3"
12d	3¼"
16d	3½"
20d	4"

Screws Though they are more expensive than nails, coated or galvanized screws offer several advantages. They do not pop out as readily as nails can, and their coating is less likely to be damaged during installation. And, with screws, you do not have to worry about hammer dents. Screws also are easier to remove than nails if a repair is required.

Galvanized deck screws are surprisingly easy to drive into softwoods such as redwood or cedar if you use a power drill or screw gun with an adjustable clutch and a Phillips screwdriver tip.

Drywall screws (so-called multipurpose screws), usually black in color, come in smaller sizes than deck screws, but their coating is not very moisture-resistant.

Galvanized and drywall screws are not rated for shear (hanging) strength, so opt for nails, lag screws, or bolts for major structural connections such as fastening rafters or posts to beams.

The lag screw (also called a lag bolt) is a heavy-duty fastener with a square or hexagonal head; it is driven into wood with a wrench or socket wrench. Before driving a lag screw, predrill a lead hole about two-thirds the length of the lag screw, using a drill bit that's ⅛ inch smaller than the lag screw's shank. Slide a washer onto a lag screw before driving it.

Choose screws that are long enough to penetrate twice the top member's thickness but not so long that they pop out the other side (for example, use 2½-inch screws to join two 2 by 4s). Screws are sold loose or in up to 25-pound boxes; the bigger the box, the lower the unit cost.

Bolts For heavy-duty fastening, choose bolts. Most are zinc-plated steel, but aluminum and brass varieties are also available. Bolts go into predrilled holes and are secured by nuts. The machine bolt has a square or hexagonal head, a nut, and two washers; it

Nails, Screws & Bolts

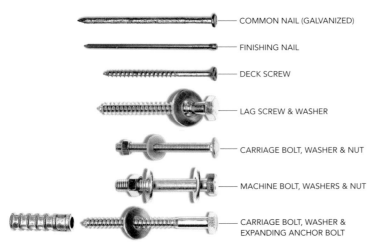

COMMON NAIL (GALVANIZED)

FINISHING NAIL

DECK SCREW

LAG SCREW & WASHER

CARRIAGE BOLT, WASHER & NUT

MACHINE BOLT, WASHERS & NUT

CARRIAGE BOLT, WASHER & EXPANDING ANCHOR BOLT

must be tightened with a wrench at each end. The carriage bolt has a self-anchoring head that digs into the wood as you tighten the nut.

Expanding anchors are designed to secure wooden members either to a masonry wall or a slab floor. They feature expanding sleeves that grip the hole firmly when you drive the bolt home.

Bolts are classified by their diameter ($\frac{1}{8}$ to 1 inch) and length ($\frac{3}{8}$ inch and up). To give the nut a firm bite, select a bolt $\frac{1}{2}$ to 1 inch longer than the combined thickness of the pieces to be joined.

It is better to make a connection using several small-diameter bolts or lag screws rather than with fewer large-diameter bolts. The number and size of fasteners needed depend on the width of the wooden members being joined.

Framing connectors Metal framing connectors are often used in construction to make joining materials easier and to make joints stronger. These connectors are used throughout almost all of this book's projects, but they are often hidden from view by wood components.

You will find many types of framing connectors in sizes that are designed to fit most standard-dimension rough and surfaced lumber. A welder or metal shop can fabricate odd sizes or decorative specialty supports.

When using framing connectors, be sure to use the size and type of nails specified by the manufacturer—these nails are generally shorter and fatter than standard nails.

Joist (and rafter) hangers, probably the most familiar metal connectors, are used to secure the butt joints between ceiling joists or rafters and the load-bearing beam, joist header, or ledger. Some joist hangers have metal prongs that can be hammered into the side of the joist (the connection to a beam must be made with nails).

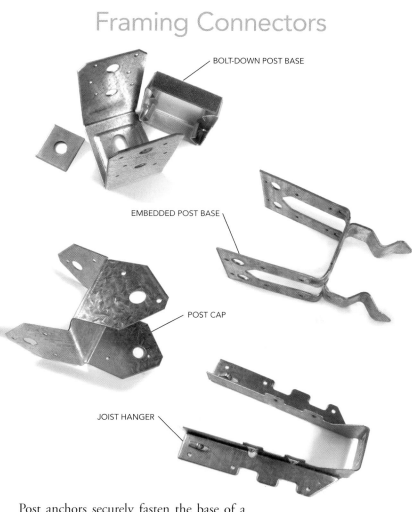

BOLT-DOWN POST BASE

EMBEDDED POST BASE

POST CAP

JOIST HANGER

Post anchors securely fasten the base of a load-bearing post to a concrete foundation, slab, or deck. In regions where there's likely to be standing water caused by heavy rains, builders typically choose an elevated post base that raises the post 1 to 3 inches above the base.

Post caps join the top of a post to a beam. They also can strengthen a splice connection between two beams.

"Framing anchors" is a catch-all term for a variety of connectors. Hurricane or seismic anchors or rafter ties eliminate the need for toenailing (joining two members together by nailing at an angle) between rafters and a wall's top plate, reinforcing angle brackets create solid joints between any two members that cross, and reinforcing straps strengthen post-to-beam joints.

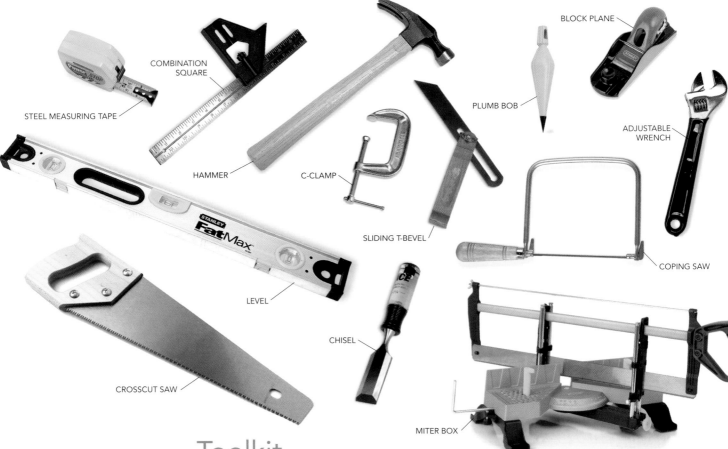

STEEL MEASURING TAPE

COMBINATION SQUARE

BLOCK PLANE

HAMMER

PLUMB BOB

C-CLAMP

ADJUSTABLE WRENCH

SLIDING T-BEVEL

COPING SAW

LEVEL

CHISEL

CROSSCUT SAW

MITER BOX

Toolkit

For building most patio roofs and gazebos, you'll need an assortment of basic carpentry tools. You won't necessarily need all of the tools discussed here, but these will handle the tasks of almost any major project. Though you can get by with hand tools for many jobs, power tools will make the work quicker, easier, and more accurate.

Hand Tools

A collection of basic tools is discussed below. If you are thinking about building your own project, you probably have most or all of these, but if you're shopping, this guide can point you in the right direction.

Chisel & block plane Though not essential, these basic carpentry tools are handy for cleaning up saw cuts and joints. A plastic-handled, metal-capped butt chisel can be driven by a hammer.

Clamp When you feel that you need an extra pair of hands, this is where a clamp comes in. Clamps hold parts to be joined where you want them, and they are also essential for bringing parts together while glue dries. C-clamps are the old standby; bar clamps have a longer reach. The spring

clamp, which looks like an oversize clothespin, is inexpensive and great for small jobs.

Coping saw Cutting curves is the coping saw's business. The wider the saw's throat, the farther in from a board's edge you can cut. An inexpensive saber saw, also known as a jigsaw, does the same type of cutting and is also easier to use and much more versatile.

Crosscut saw This tool is merely a handsaw that's designed to cut boards across their widths. It can be handy for cutting where a power saw's cord doesn't easily reach, and it is much safer than using a power saw when you're working at the top of a ladder. A good choice is a 26-inch blade with 8 points per inch. For finer work, a backsaw, which is stiffer than a crosscut saw and has finer teeth, will do the job better.

Hammer Have a 16-ounce, curved-claw hammer for general work and a 20-ounce straight-claw model for framing.

Level A carpenter's level helps check parts of a structure for both level and plumb. To check level across a very long distance, use a line level, or consider buying a laser level or a water level.

Miter box Made from wood, metal, or plastic, this trough-like frame has various slots in its sides to guide the saw blade for accurately cutting angles.

Plumb bob Most overheads require a reference point in order to line up posts or transfer layout lines from the ground to overhead beams. To accomplish this work, you'll want a plumb bob and mason's line.

Square An adjustable combination square helps you draw straight lines across lumber to be cut, check cuts for square, check angles on assembled pieces of a structure, and handle a variety of other layout tasks. A sliding T-bevel helps you lay out and transfer angles for cutting.

Steel measuring tape For your outdoor construction work, have one that is 1 inch wide and 25 feet long.

Wrench An adjustable wrench is good for turning or holding bolt heads and nuts. A ratchet-and-socket set is easier to use, particularly for reaching into a countersunk bolt hole while tightening the bolt.

Power Tools

The following portable power tools make large projects go more quickly and easily; in the hands of an adept do-it-yourselfer, they also produce more professional results than hand tools. In addition to the power tools listed here, such larger, stationary power tools as a table saw, radial-arm saw, and band saw will make short order of certain stages of building an overhead or gazebo.

Electric drill & bits This power tool has all but replaced hand drills and screwdrivers when more than a couple of screws are involved. Look for a $^3/_8$-inch cordless reversible drill. To bore holes up to $^1/_2$ inch in diameter, use standard twist bits; for larger holes, use spade bits.

A carbide-tipped masonry bit can drill into stucco siding with no problem. When fitted with a Phillips-head tip, the drill is equally handy as a power screwdriver, but you'll need a variable-speed model or the screws will strip. Models with an adjustable clutch prevent screws from being driven too deep.

Miter saw Also called a chop saw, the miter saw is the power version of the good old backsaw and miter box. It excels at making clean, accurate angle cuts—a dream for projects that entail a lot of angles or require a lot of detail work. A 10-inch miter saw is standard. So-called compound miter saws cut angles in two directions at once, a feature that's sometimes handy for rafters or fancy trim. Sliding miter saws can cut stock up to about a foot wide.

SABER SAW

ELECTRIC DRILL & BITS

PORTABLE CIRCULAR SAW

RECIPROCATING SAW

MITER SAW

ROUTER

using this tool. This saw is also helpful for cutting off pieces in cramped locations and, when equipped with a metal-cutting blade, for cutting steel reinforcing bar.

Router The electric router makes quick work of grooves, rabbets (grooves along an edge), and the decorative edge treatments—chamfers (bevels) and roundovers (rounded edges), for example—that can spice up a basic project. Look for a router rated at least 1 horsepower.

Portable circular saw This does the same job as a handsaw but much more quickly and effortlessly. Equipped with a combination blade, it can handle all types of cuts. The 7¼-inch size is standard.

Reciprocating saw A reciprocating saw, with its long blade, can cut much thicker pieces of wood than can a standard circular saw. If you are installing 6-by-6 posts, you will be able to cut them to length quickly

Saber saw The power version of the coping saw, a saber saw, or jigsaw, can be used for both straight and delicately curved cuts. Unlike a coping saw, the saber saw can make cuts well away from an edge, and it even makes interior "pocket" cuts when you drill an access hole first. Choose the right blade for the job. Thin, fine-tooth blades are perfect for tight curves, and beefier ones work for rougher, straighter cuts.

Working Safely

Before you begin work, make sure you have the necessary safety equipment. Wear goggles or safety glasses when operating power tools or using any striking tool. Wear a respirator to avoid breathing harmful vapors (such as those from oil-based finishes). Use a disposable painter's dust mask to protect against breathing-in sawdust; it's essential when you are cutting pressure-treated lumber. Also wear earmuff hearing protectors or earplugs when you are operating power tools for any length of time. A hard hat should always be worn when you're working beneath an overhead or with others in close quarters.

Wear all-leather or leather-reinforced cotton work gloves when handling wood; wear rubber gloves when applying finishes or other caustic products. Sturdy work boots, especially the steel-toed sort, will protect your feet from dropped tools or lumber.

When using a new tool, always read the owner's manual carefully and follow all safety directions. To guard against shock, make sure power tools are either double-insulated or grounded. Double-insulated tools, which contain a built-in second barrier of protective insulation, offer the best protection; they are clearly marked and should not be grounded (they have two-pronged plugs only).

Because a good deal of your work will likely transpire outdoors, take special precautions against shock. A ground-fault circuit interrupter (GFCI), either portable or built into the outlet, will cut electricity to your power tools with lightning speed if there's a leak in current.

Building Tips

Even if you have basic carpentry skills, here you'll find a few special techniques that can make the going easier. If you are inexperienced in working with wood, it's best to hire a professional.

Cutting With Saws

Every project in this book involves cutting wood. Listed below are a few helpful tips for the types of cutting techniques involved in building outdoor structures.

Cutting straight Whether you're using hand tools or portable power tools, it can be difficult to get a really straight cut. One solution is to clamp a guide onto the piece you're cutting; any straight board or plywood piece with a straight edge can guide your handsaw or the shoe of your portable circular saw. If you're using a power saw, first figure out the distance from the edge of the saw's shoe to its blade, and then space the straightedge this distance from the line you are cutting. Be sure to cut to the waste side of your line.

Cutting deep Cutting entirely through a 4-by-4 post can be awkward, at best. If you're using a handsaw, first mark the cutting line across the board, and then, guiding the pencil with your square, extend this line down both sides. Use the side lines to keep your saw on track. If you are using a circular saw, you can only cut about half the depth of the board at once. Finish making the cut with a

handsaw, using the existing cut as a guide. Or, better yet, flip the 4 by 4 over, and make a second cut from the bottom, carefully matching saw cuts (see page 70).

Cutting angles To cut angles, first mark the cut line using a sliding T-bevel. If the angle is a standard one, such as 30 degrees or 45 degrees, you can cut it using a miter box and handsaw. Otherwise, either cut it freehand with a circular saw, or clamp on a guide, allowing for the distance from base plate to blade. It is easiest to cut odd angles with a power miter saw.

Cutting curves Cut curves freehand with either a coping saw or a power saber saw. If a curve is uniform, lay it out using a compass or a French curve or by plotting it on paper. Then cut it out to make a template. If you are making more than one matching piece, as with decorative rafter tails or knee braces, cut the first one to your satisfaction, and then use it to lay out the rest.

Decorative cutting Decorative details are best done with an electric router. Most edge details—such as chamfers, rabbets, and

For 45-degree and 90-degree cuts across small stock, a miter box and handsaw are easy and efficient tool choices.

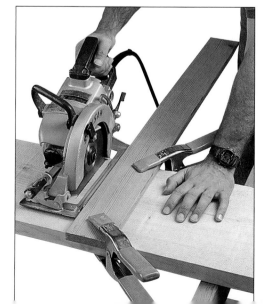

Left: A circular saw with a straightedge guide helps create clean and straight cuts. Right: A saber saw makes cutting curves a cinch.

A router is indispensable for decorative edge detailing. Shown above from top to bottom are chamfer, rabbet, and roundover edges.

roundovers—are fashioned with corresponding bits; these all come with pilot bushings that guide the bit along an edge. Do this sort of detailing before assembling the structure. You can also cut rabbets using a table saw and dado blade.

Basic Joinery

Most patio roof and gazebo projects call for simple butt joints; trim pieces are sometimes mitered or lapped. These three main joints are shown in the photographs below.

Butt joints This type of joint has standard 90-degree ends. If one piece overlaps the other, driving nails or screws is easy. However, if the pieces join in a T and you can't drive fasteners from behind, joining them can be awkward. Traditional "toenailing" can be exasperating, since the part being secured tends to move off-line as you hammer. Screws are a bit easier to work with, especially if you drill angled pilot holes first. Clamps and blocks can also hold pieces in

line. But framing connectors or L-brackets are easier to use at these junctions, and they also make for a stronger joint. If you don't like the way they look, paint them with a concealing or complementary color.

Miter joints Cut at 45-degree angles, end miters (like those at the corners of picture frames) are pretty straightforward. Edge miters (along the lengths of boards) are difficult to cut by hand unless the stock is narrow enough to fit upright in a miter box; otherwise, use a sliding or compound miter saw, radial-arm saw, or table saw. You can also use a circular saw's bevel (side-tilt) adjustment, but cuts made this way are often imprecise.

Lap joints This type of joint calls for other techniques. A half-lap has a notch or groove cut in one piece, and the other piece sits inside the notch. A full-lap joint, where both pieces are of equal thickness, joins corresponding notches, each one-half the total depth. Though it certainly can be done with

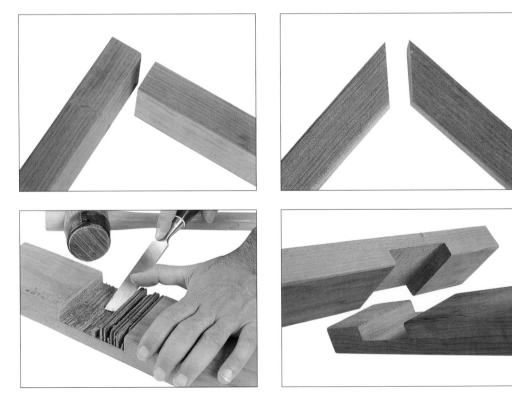

Clockwise from top left are a butt joint, miter joint, and lap joint; the notch in a lap joint can be made using a radial-arm saw and dado blade, a portable circular saw and chisel, or a handsaw and chisel.

a handsaw and chisel, it is demanding work. To cut with a portable circular saw, set the blade's depth at one-half the piece's depth. Make two cuts to outline the joint's shoulder, and then make several more cuts in the "waste area" between the lines, as shown at bottom left on the opposite page. Use a sharp chisel, with its bevel pointed downward, to remove the waste and smooth the joint's bottom. A radial-arm saw and a dado blade are the best tools to cut these joints.

Drilling for Fasteners

In certain situations, and especially where a fastener will be highly visible, you will need to drill a clean, straight hole. The most common problems that occur are that the hole may not be exactly perpendicular and the back side of the hole (where the drill bit exits the wood) may splinter.

Drilling straight You can usually drill a fairly straight hole simply by eyeballing the drill bit's angle as you go. To be precise, place a square next to the drill.

Preventing splintering You can solve the problem of ragged exit holes in two ways. One is to temporarily attach a wood scrap behind the joint and drill through the main piece and into the scrap. The other is to drill most of the way through the piece and stop when the bit's tip starts to protrude. Then flip over the piece and finish drilling from the back side.

Drilling pilot holes Deck and drywall screws have sharp points and aggressive threads, so you shouldn't need to drill pilot holes to drive them into redwood or other softwoods. But if the screws are not cooperating, or they split the wood when driven near a board's end, choose a drill bit slightly smaller than the screw, and drill a pilot hole about three-quarters of the screw's length.

If you want your machine bolts countersunk, first drill a large, shallow hole for the fastener's head, and then drill a smaller hole clear through the wood for the shank.

Countersinking A finished project often looks better if lag screws and machine bolts are countersunk (when their heads are driven below the wood's surface). Use a spade bit to bore the countersunk hole for the head; size it just slightly larger than the fastener's washer, and drill just deeper than the length of the fastener's head. Then drill a second, smaller pilot hole for the fastener, boring through the center of the countersunk hole. When using lag screws, make this second pilot hole the same diameter as the smooth shank between the screw threads and the head. Drill the hole to a depth of about two-thirds the length of the screw.

Driving lag screws & bolts Start the lag screw with a few hammer blows, and then drive it tight with a wrench or ratchet. If it won't go in, make the pilot hole longer.

For bolts, drill a hole just slightly larger than the shank (the bolt must slide freely inside it) all the way through the joint. Use two wrenches to secure a machine bolt: one on the head and another on the nut to keep the bolt from twirling. Carriage bolts require just one wrench, on the nut; the head should stay put.

Installing a Ledger

A house-attached patio roof takes advantage of the house's structure by supporting one end of the roof on a ledger mounted horizontally to the house. The ledger, typically a 2 by 6, is usually designed to hold one end of the patio roof rafters. Locating and mounting the ledger is normally a fairly easy process; the ledger should be attached before the foundation is built.

Locating the ledger On a one-story house, it is often best to attach the ledger just below the eaves. On a two-story house, you can usually tie into a band joist (also called a rim joist) located between the floors, as shown below. Find the band joist by measuring down from a second-story window.

Mounting the ledger Procedures for mounting a ledger depend on the type of siding on the house.

Relatively flat siding can remain intact, but clapboard, beveled wood, metal, or vinyl siding should always be cut away to allow a solid connection point for the ledger. If you have beveled horizontal siding, then use an inverted piece of siding, as shown in the top illustration below left to create a plumb surface for attaching the ledger. If your siding is not beveled, you can simply screw the ledger tightly to it.

Remove enough of the siding so you can tuck flashing behind the siding above the ledger and allow it to overhang the siding below the ledger.

When cutting wood siding, adjust the blade of the circular saw so it cuts just the siding and not the sheathing underneath. Also, do not let the blade cut beyond the layout lines. If you are cutting vinyl siding, you can use a sharp utility knife instead.

A ledger should be affixed to strong parts of the house's framing, such as second-floor joists or wall studs. The strongest ledger connection relies on bolts that run through the ledger and the house sheathing and rim joist and then are fastened with nuts and washers affixed from the other side. When access to the other side of the fasteners is unfeasible, use lag screws instead of bolts. If it is impossible to attach the ledger to a floor joist, then fasten the ledger to wall studs, which are generally located on 16-inch (or sometimes 24-inch) centers and doubled up around doors, windows, and other openings.

Temporarily nail or brace the ledger in place, positioned and leveled at the desired height. Recheck for level, and then drill lag-screw or bolt pilot holes through the ledger and into the house's framing. Attach the ledger with ½-inch-diameter lag screws or bolts every 16 inches (or as specified by local building codes).

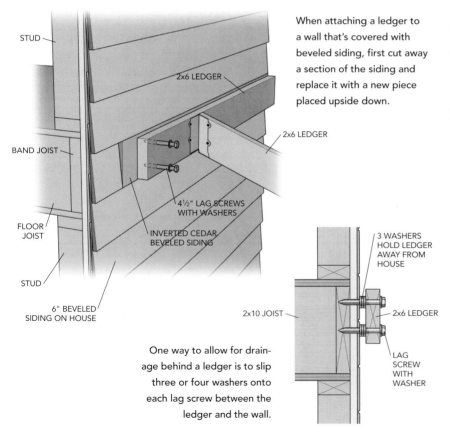

STUD

2x6 LEDGER

When attaching a ledger to a wall that's covered with beveled siding, first cut away a section of the siding and replace it with a new piece placed upside down.

2x6 LEDGER

BAND JOIST

4½" LAG SCREWS WITH WASHERS

FLOOR JOIST

INVERTED CEDAR BEVELED SIDING

STUD

6" BEVELED SIDING ON HOUSE

One way to allow for drainage behind a ledger is to slip three or four washers onto each lag screw between the ledger and the wall.

2x10 JOIST

3 WASHERS HOLD LEDGER AWAY FROM HOUSE

2x6 LEDGER

LAG SCREW WITH WASHER

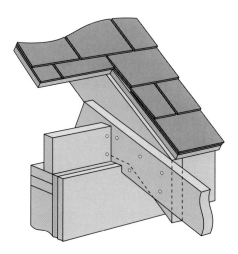

To allow maximum headroom, rafters for a patio roof can be supported by the wall's top plate and nailed to the sides of the primary roof rafters.

Slip three or four stainless-steel washers between the ledger and the siding when driving each screw. This will allow water to flow behind the ledger.

If attaching a patio roof to a ledger beneath the eaves does not allow for enough headroom, you can set the new patio roof's rafters on the wall's top plate and fasten them to the sides of the house rafters, as shown in the cutaway drawing above.

Fastening to masonry walls Anchor a ledger to a masonry wall with expanding anchor bolts. Begin by marking a line across the wall for the ledger's top edge. Drill holes for the expanding anchors every 16 inches or as specified by local codes, insert the anchors, hold the ledger in place, and tap it with a hammer to indent the anchor locations on its back face. Remove the ledger, and drill bolt holes where the bolt tips have left marks. Push or hammer the ledger back onto the bolts, recheck for level (making any needed adjustments), add washers and nuts, and then tighten the bolts.

Flashing a ledger Unless it will be protected from rain by the house's eaves or a solid roof, a roof ledger that is fastened directly to a house with wood siding should be capped with galvanized metal flashing and caulked, as shown at bottom, to prevent water from seeping in behind it. This is a job you must do before fastening the overhead's roof rafters in place.

You can buy L- or Z-shaped flashing or bend it yourself. To bend sheet-metal flashing, make a form by clamping two 2 by 4s together on each side of the metal, and then hammer the metal to create a sharp edge at each fold. Fit the flashing in place, caulk the top edge, and nail it with galvanized nails long enough to penetrate at least 1 inch into the structural members. Then caulk the nail heads. If the house is sided with shingles or lap siding, simply slip the metal's top edge up under the bottom edge of the shingles or siding as far as possible.

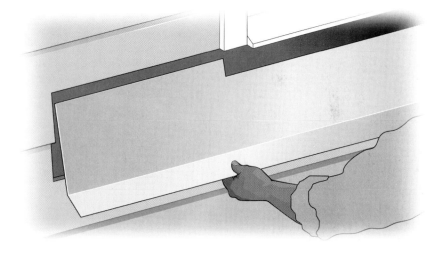

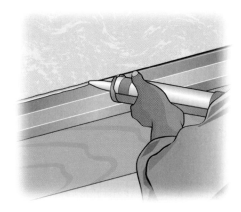

Before attaching a ledger, tuck sheet-metal flashing up under the siding (above). Where integral flashing isn't possible, such as on a stucco wall, use Z-flashing and caulk the top edge (left).

The Foundation

Patio roofs and gazebos are typically supported by a foundation—either a concrete slab such as an existing patio or a series of footings and piers. The foundation distributes the structure's weight and anchors it against settling, erosion, and wind lift. The foundation also isolates the posts or walls from direct contact with the ground, mitigating the chance of decay from moisture and insect infestation.

Typically, a foundation's footing must extend into solid ground or rock. In cold-climate areas, it must extend below the frost line so that it is not disturbed by frost heave. Foundation requirements are set by local codes; a steel-reinforced concrete footing that extends 6 inches below the frost line, as shown on page 66, is typical for patio roofs and gazebos with built-up floors.

The footing supports a poured-in-place or precast concrete pier, which in turn supports a post. The placement of footings and piers is dependent upon the post locations, which in turn are determined by the beam and rafter spans. For more about these, see page 49.

Building on a Slab or Deck

If local codes allow setting the overhead directly on an existing slab but the concrete is not thick enough to support the overhead's weight, you will have to pour new footings around the slab's perimeter or break out sections and pour deeper footings.

Building over an existing slab To fasten an overhead directly to an existing slab, secure each post in a post anchor. For example, in some areas, a new structure can stand on a concrete slab if the slab is a minimum $3\frac{1}{2}$ inches thick and the structure's posts do not support combined "live" and "dead" loads in excess of 750 pounds per post ("live" loads are forces from wind, people, and so forth; "dead" loads are from the weight of the structure itself). Standard post anchors are sized to work with rough and surfaced 4-by-4, 4-by-6, and 6-by-6 posts (other sizes can be specially fabricated).

For each post, drill a hole in the concrete with a masonry bit, centered for the anchor, to receive a $\frac{1}{2}$-inch expanding anchor bolt. Insert the anchor bolt, place the post anchor, add a washer and nut, and tighten with a wrench. When it's time to place the post, cut the end square, sit it in the stirrup of the base, and nail the anchor to the post through prepunched holes.

Another very strong option is to fasten the post anchor with a short piece of threaded

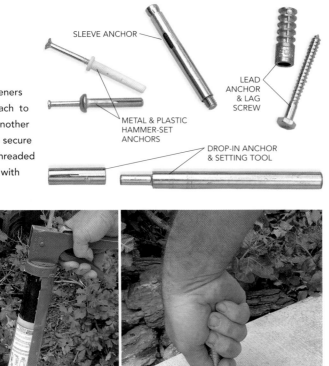

SLEEVE ANCHOR

LEAD ANCHOR & LAG SCREW

METAL & PLASTIC HAMMER-SET ANCHORS

DROP-IN ANCHOR & SETTING TOOL

Right: Several fasteners can be used to attach to masonry. Below: Another strong option is to secure a short length of threaded rod in a hole filled with epoxy cement.

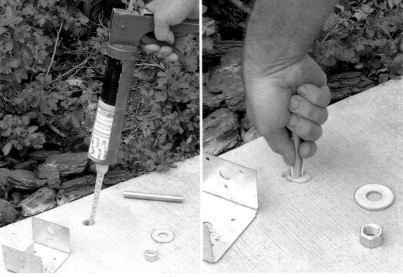

rod that you secure in a hole with epoxy cement. Mark the anchor's placement, and use a masonry bit to drill a hole that's slightly wider than the threaded rod. Next, blow out all remaining dust, and fill the hole with epoxy. Immediately insert a threaded rod to the desired depth, and allow the epoxy to set until it is rock-solid (this may take all day). Then add the anchor, slide a washer onto the rod, and tighten the nut down.

Building on an existing deck If you are allowed by local building codes, you can bolt your new structure's posts to existing deck beams, joists, or other heavy structural members. The type of post base discussed previously can be lag-screwed through decking to a joist or beam. Be sure to use lag screws that are long enough to penetrate the structural member by at least 2 inches.

Ideally, gazebos and garden rooms that have wooden deck-like floors are very low to the ground. You can usually lower the height of a floor by using smaller-width joists and beams. However, this change may require you to reduce beam and joist spans, which in

turn may mean pouring more footings. Another strategy is to attach the joists to the side, not the top, of the beam. See three options in the illustrations below left.

If the yard is level and the floor will be low to the ground, you will not need posts. However, the piers must all be level with one another. To build with no posts, plan to install at least two rows of piers with identical beams placed along each row. Construct the beams with double 2-by members. Attach joists with joist hangers on the inside face of each beam.

When mounting posts on an existing deck, soundly bolt them to the deck's heaviest structural members.

With a ground-hugging deck floor for a gazebo structure, treated-wood floor joists can be mounted directly on piers.

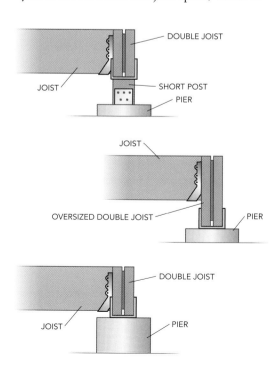

DOUBLE JOIST

JOIST

SHORT POST

PIER

JOIST

OVERSIZED DOUBLE JOIST

PIER

DOUBLE JOIST

JOIST

PIER

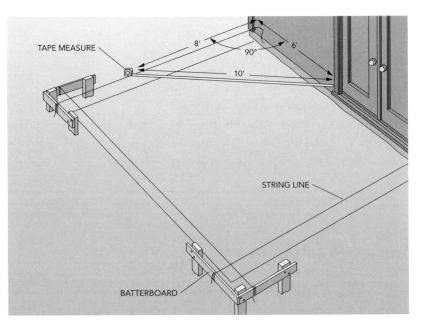

TAPE MEASURE

8'

90°

6'

10'

STRING LINE

BATTERBOARD

Lay out the perimeter of your project by tying taut string lines to batterboards. Use the 3-4-5 rule (above right) to make sure the layout is 90 degrees at the corners. Use a plumb bob to establish the ledger's location at ground level (see below).

Siting the Project

Transfer the size and layout of your overhead's foundation to the ground, deck, or patio. For marking the ground, use powdered chalk or drive stakes into the ground. To mark a deck or patio, use a carpenter's pencil or crayon.

For precise placement of footings, set up batterboards, as shown above. These will allow you to adjust and maintain taut perimeter lines while digging the footing holes. Batterboards are temporary attachment points for string lines. They are usually made with 1 by 4s or 2 by 4s, but you can use any scrap lumber available. Each batterboard consists of a crosspiece mounted on two stakes, which are cut with pointed bottoms so they can be driven easily into the ground.

If you are building off a house wall, run a plumb line down from each end of the ledger and drive a nail partially into the wall just above ground level, or you can set up batterboards at the base of the wall and then drive in a nail at the plumb bob's location. Run mason's lines from the nails to the opposite batterboards and then parallel to the wall from batterboard to batterboard, as shown in the illustration at left.

For a house-attached overhead, partially drive a second small nail into the siding exactly 3 feet away (see the illustration above). Hook the end of one tape measure onto one nail and the end of another tape measure onto the other nail. With a helper, pull out the tapes until the 4-foot mark on one tape meets the 5-foot mark on the other

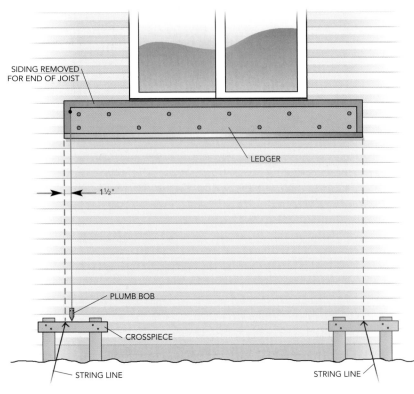

SIDING REMOVED FOR END OF JOIST

LEDGER

1½"

PLUMB BOB

CROSSPIECE

STRING LINE

STRING LINE

tape to be sure the layout is perfectly perpendicular to the wall.

Use the same method for a freestanding structure, but pound stakes into the ground instead of a nail into the siding. This triangulation method works in any multiple of 3-4-5: for example, 6-8-10, 9-12-15, and so on. For maximum accuracy, use the largest ratio possible.

To double-check for square, measure the diagonal distances between opposite corners. If necessary, adjust the lines until both measurements match. When locating footing and post locations this way, remember that these lines show the perimeter—not the centers—of the posts and footings.

Buying or Mixing Concrete

For footings and/or a slab, you will need concrete. Basic concrete is composed of Portland cement, sand, gravel (also called aggregate), and water. Portland cement is the glue that holds the mix together. The more cement there is, the stronger the concrete will be. If you are mixing a small amount of concrete or mortar and want to strengthen it, simply add a shovel or two of cement. When ordering from a ready-mix company, specify how much cement you want; a "six-bag mix" contains six bags of cement per yard of concrete, making it strong enough for most projects. For more about the proper mixture of concrete, see "Mixing your own" on the following page.

If you live in an area with freezing winters, consider ordering air-entrained concrete, which contains tiny bubbles. The bubbles lend the concrete a bit of flexibility, so it is less likely to crack in cold weather. Air-entrained concrete is available only from a concrete truck.

If freezing weather is possible on the day of the pour, you can order an accelerating additive, which makes the concrete harden more quickly. If the weather is hot and dry, think about adding a retardant, which will slow the drying time. If the concrete sets too quickly, you may not have enough time to correctly finish the surface.

Ordering guidelines Begin by taking careful measurements of the area to be filled with concrete. A discrepancy of only ½ inch can make a big difference in the amount of concrete you will need.

When ordering, tell the supplier the square footage and depth. A reliable supplier will calculate how much you will need, but you want to double-check these calculations against your own.

Concrete is usually sold by the cubic yard, just called a yard. A yard of concrete (or sand or gravel) fills an area 3 feet by 3 feet by 3 feet. For a small project, such as a pier footing, you may choose to measure cubic footage instead; bags of dry-mix concrete often include cubic footage measurements on the package.

It is very easy to figure out concrete needs. For a footing or for a rectangular slab, simply multiply the width in feet times the length in feet times the thickness in inches. Divide the result by 12 to get the number of cubic feet. Divide that number by 27 to get the cubic yards. For example, if a slab measures 20 feet by 30 feet and its thickness is 3½ inches:

20 x 30 x 3.5 = 2,100

2,100 ÷ 12 = 175 cubic feet

175 ÷ 27 = 6.48 yards

Adding about 10 percent for waste, you would order a little more than 7 yards.

If you need more than ¼ yard of concrete, ordering ready-mixed concrete is in almost all cases worth the extra expense. A 60-pound

For mixing small amounts of concrete, you can rent an electric concrete mixer.

Once a concrete truck arrives, you must work quickly. Be sure all forms are ready, reinforcing steel is placed, and tools are at the site.

- Run and test wheelbarrow paths, install all forms and guides, and make sure they are securely anchored.
- If required, make sure the building inspector has checked the site before you pour.
- If your design includes metal post anchors that will be embedded in the slab, have them on hand.

Mixing your own If you want to mix concrete in small batches or are unable to find a company that will do that for you, you can rent an electric-powered concrete mixer. Transporting the sand, gravel, and bagged cement requires a pickup truck with a bed that seals tight.

To mix your own concrete for footings and piers, use 1 part Portland cement, 2 parts clean river sand, and 3 parts gravel (maximum of 1 inch diameter and specially washed for concrete mixing). Add clean water, a little at a time, as you mix. The concrete should be plastic and not runny. You can also use dry mix or transit mix, which contain the same proportions of cement, sand, and gravel detailed above. Tumble, adding water slowly for two to three minutes, and then pour.

Concrete hardens because the powder-like cement and water form an adhesive that binds the sand and gravel together. Too much water thins or dilutes this adhesive paste and weakens its cementing qualities; too little makes it stiff and unworkable.

If the batch is too stiff, add water one cup at a time and continue mixing until it's right. If it is too soupy, add small amounts of sand and gravel. Note that concrete changes consistency radically when you add even small amounts of any ingredient.

Pouring a Concrete Foundation

Following are typical methods of pouring concrete foundations. Be aware that the

sack of dry-mix concrete makes around ½ cubic foot, meaning that you would need to mix 52 bags to make one yard of concrete.

Many ready-mix-concrete companies will not deliver less than a yard of concrete. Others have special trucks designed to mix smaller amounts at the job site. If one company won't deliver a small amount for you, just keep calling around.

Before the truck arrives Before you arrange for concrete to be delivered, familiarize yourself with the steps on pages 66–67; you won't have time to read instructions once the work begins. If the truck driver has to wait more than half an hour, you usually will incur extra expense, so plan to move the concrete quickly.

- Have all the necessary tools on hand, including two wheelbarrows.
- Be ready with at least one reliable helper, preferably two.
- If you want a smooth steel-trowel finish, line up an experienced concrete finisher.
- Install any isolation joints as well as wire reinforcement beforehand.

foundations of some patio roof or gazebo structures are integrated into the foundation of a patio or deck. For example, when a concrete patio is poured, deeper footings may be poured around the slab's perimeter to support the structure. In the case of decks, structural members such as railing supports may be sized long enough to support the roof of the overhead.

In many areas, you will need a building permit to pour a concrete foundation or slab. Check with your local building department, and be sure to follow the inspector's instructions to the letter.

Before doing the following work, read the section on "Buying or Mixing Concrete" on pages 63–64.

Footings & piers Waxed fiber tubes, readily available at home improvement centers and lumberyards, make forming and pouring footings and piers a relatively easy job. Be aware that, by some codes, you may be required to have the footings inspected before making the piers, or you may need to add several inches of gravel to the bottom of each footing before adding concrete.

Dig and pour all footings and piers at one time, if possible. Have rebar and anchor bolts or post bases on hand, as you must add them to the concrete while it is still wet.

Lay out the footings as discussed on page 62. The spacing between footings for support posts is determined by post placements, which are a factor of beam spans (see the chart on page 49).

In areas with freezing winters, a concrete footing usually must extend at least 12 inches below the frost line (the depth at which soil freezes). A footing should also be at minimum 8 inches thick and twice as wide as the wall or posts it will support.

Begin by digging a flared hole, sized as required by code, using a clamshell digger or a power hole auger. Cut a length of waxed fiber tube (in some cases, fiber tubes can be difficult to locate; instead, you can form rectangular footings from scrap plywood or wood) long enough to extend 2 inches above grade and 2 inches into the flared footing at the bottom of the hole. Level and suspend this tube in the center of the hole by screwing it to temporary braces.

Next, fill the flared section of the footing and the bottom 2 feet of the tube with concrete. Using a piece of wood, agitate the mix to remove any air pockets. Repeat the process every 2 feet, until the tube is slightly overfilled. Smooth the surface by moving a short 2 by 4 from side to side across the top.

Add rebar according to code requirements, typically two pieces of #4 rebar spaced about 2 inches from the fiber tube. Each should be

To cast a footing, use a spade to transfer concrete into the hole and fiber-tube form. Using a thin scrap of wood, poke the concrete repeatedly to release any trapped air. Smooth the surface with a short 2 by 4, add any necessary rebar, and then position and level the post anchor.

An alternative method of anchoring a post is to drill a deep hole into its bottom end and slip it down over a pipe that's embedded in the concrete footing.

A common foundation type for outdoor structures consists of a concrete footing with a precast pier positioned while the footing is still plastic.

long enough to reach from the bottom of the footing to about 2 inches below the pier's surface. Insert an anchor bolt, post base, or short rebar "pin" for centering the post, and check it for alignment.

Another option is to push a long ¾-inch-diameter galvanized pipe into the center of the wet footing, leaving about 16 inches sticking up. You then drill an 18-inch-deep hole into the bottom of each post so you can slip the post down onto the pipe. Though this requires a very long drill bit and drilling a straight hole into the post's bottom, assembly of the structure is easier because, with most designs, posts can stand unsupported while you fasten other members to them.

Depending upon the type and size of project you are building, you may be able to set a

ready-made concrete pier on a footing. Choose the type of piers with integral metal post anchors. Soak the piers with a hose, and then place them on the footings five to 10 minutes after the footings have been poured, when the concrete is stiff enough to support them. Then, with the post anchors properly aligned with your string lines, level the piers in both directions.

Keep the concrete damp for two days, allowing it to cure slowly. Then remove the temporary braces, backfill the hole with dirt, and cut away the exposed fiber tubing.

How to Pour a Slab

A concrete slab may be cast at the same time as footings or after the footings have set up. The slab's overall dimensions are determined by the size of your new structure.

Before casting a concrete slab, first place any plumbing or electrical conduit that will run under or through it. After casting the slab, do not allow the surface to dry too quickly or it may crack. Spray it with a light mist of water, cover it with plastic sheeting, and allow it to cure for three days (longer in cold weather).

Begin by marking the slab's placement on the ground with powdered chalk, or stretch mason's lines between batterboards (see page 62) to determine the perimeter of the foundation. A rectangular slab should have corners at precise 90-degree angles. To ensure the corners are square, lay out a triangle with sides 3 feet, 4 feet, and 5 feet long as discussed on pages 62–63.

Excavate a flat-bottomed hole for a 4-inch-thick slab; in areas where frost or drainage may be a problem, the slab should be poured over a 4-to-6-inch gravel bed, so dig deeply enough to accommodate this.

Build temporary forms from scrap lumber nailed securely to stakes. Make sure the top edges of the forms are level to expedite finishing the concrete later. Pour the gravel bed.

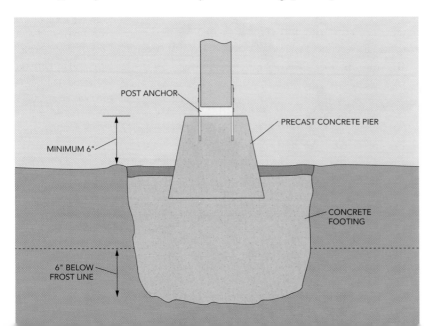

POST ANCHOR

PRECAST CONCRETE PIER

MINIMUM 6"

CONCRETE FOOTING

6" BELOW FROST LINE

Reinforce the area as required by code (typically with ½-inch reinforcing bar around the perimeter and 6-inch-square N. 10-10 welded-wire mesh within the slab area). Support the mesh about 2 inches above the base with small pieces of brick or block.

Thoroughly dampen the soil or gravel. Then, beginning at one corner, place and spread the concrete. Work the mix up against the form, and compact it into all corners with a shovel or mortar hoe by pushing (not dragging) it. Don't overwork the material or the heavy aggregate may sink to the bottom.

With a helper, move a straight 2 by 4 across the top of the forms to level the concrete, using a zigzag, sawing motion. Fill any voids with more concrete and relevel.

To smooth the surface, move a darby (which you may want to rent) in overlapping arcs, and then in overlapping straight, side-to-side strokes. Keep the tool flat—don't let it dig in. After the water sheen disappears from the concrete, but before the surface becomes really stiff, smooth it once more with a wood or magnesium hand float.

While the concrete is still plastic, install anchor bolts where required by your plan, typically every 3 to 4 feet.

Clockwise from top left: After installing the gravel bed, add reinforcing bar and welded-wire mesh. Pour the concrete, work it into the form, and then use a long 2 by 4 to screed the concrete level with the tops of the forms. Fill any voids, and then use a darby to smooth the surface. Install anchor bolts before the concrete sets.

Posts & Beams

The main structural members of patio and deck overheads are posts or columns and beams, which run from post to post or from post to ledger. The beams support the roof rafters or joists, which in turn hold the roofing material. Minimum sizes of posts and beams are set by engineering requirements and are strictly governed by local building codes.

Before beginning construction, consider finishing all of the lumber you will be using (see page 88). In most cases, it's much easier to apply a finish to the lumber when it's sitting on sawhorses than when you're standing on top of a ladder. If you prefinish the wood, plan to touch it up after construction is complete.

Posts & Columns

As discussed on pages 32–33, posts and columns may be made from several types of materials. Here we look at the most common: solid lumber such as 4 by 4s, 6 by 6s, and 8 by 8s. Sometimes, they're built up from more than one size of lumber. Any post that will touch the ground should be pressure-treated for decay resistance. Posts offer plenty of latitude for detailing—you can rout them, cut them, build up interesting profiles, or nail on decorative pieces to add visual interest.

Beams

Beams can be solid lumber or can be built from lengths of 2-by lumber nailed together with $\frac{1}{2}$-inch pressure-treated plywood spacers in between (this forms a $3\frac{1}{2}$-inch-thick beam that is equal to the width of a 4-by post). A built-up beam is easiest to handle because you can assemble it near its final destination, but making one involves a little more labor. In highly visible areas, a single, solid beam generally looks better.

You can also build up a 3-inch-wide beam without spacers. Just nail together the two boards by driving 10d galvanized nails along both sides every 16 inches, staggering them as shown at bottom left. Apply a bead of silicone caulk to the joint between the boards to prevent moisture from seeping between them. Be sure the crowns (the "high" side of a curve or warp along the edge of a board) on the pieces align; then, when you mount the beam on the posts, place the crown side up.

If you must assemble a long, built-up beam from shorter lengths, stagger the joints between successive layers and plan for each of these joints to fall directly over a post.

Some designs use paired 2-by joists to substitute for beams. The project on page 132, for example, utilizes two 2 by 8s with a space in between to provide the main support for rafters and lattice roofing. Generally speaking, these partnered beams have a less weighty, airier appearance and are easier to handle than a single beam.

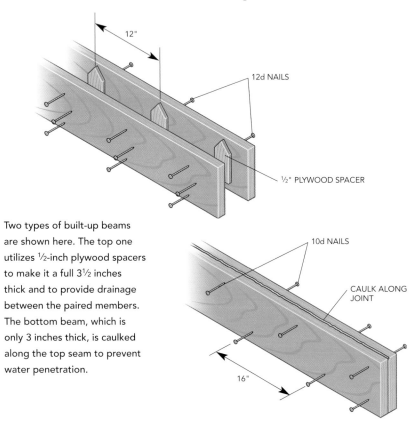

12"

12d NAILS

$\frac{1}{2}$" PLYWOOD SPACER

10d NAILS

CAULK ALONG JOINT

16"

Two types of built-up beams are shown here. The top one utilizes $\frac{1}{2}$-inch plywood spacers to make it a full $3\frac{1}{2}$ inches thick and to provide drainage between the paired members. The bottom beam, which is only 3 inches thick, is caulked along the top seam to prevent water penetration.

Erecting Posts & Beams

Accurately measuring post heights is critical when building an overhead; you cannot achieve a stable, properly aligned substructure without precise post measurements. The construction examples that are discussed here are for attached overheads with beams and rafters; if your design is different, adjust the directions accordingly.

For a house-attached overhead, measure, cut, and erect the posts that are farthest from the house first. For a freestanding roof, begin with the corners, and then erect all of the intermediate posts.

Measuring posts for a freestanding roof differs in only one respect from measuring for a house-attached roof: With the attached roof, you've already defined the roof height at the ledger line. For a freestanding overhead, you will need to erect a post slightly taller than the desired height, mark the height on the post, and work from it as you would from a ledger. The minimum clearance for beams in an occupied space is normally 7 feet to prevent people from bumping their heads.

Left: To hold the post in position, utilize stakes and temporary diagonal braces.

Check both the front and side of a post for plumb, and then temporarily nail the post to a supporting brace.

This innovative level is made to help when you are erecting posts—it has bubbles on two sides so you can check for plumb in both directions at once. You affix it to the post with a large rubber band.

Measuring & marking posts Begin by cutting the posts 6 to 12 inches longer than the finish length. Have a helper hold the first post plumb on its anchor. If you are using pressure-treated posts, make sure to place the uncut end into the post base—but only if it is square. Use a combination square to check; if the post isn't square, cut just enough off the bottom to make it square. Coat the cut surface with a water-repellent preservative before setting the post in place.

Posts can be quite heavy, so you'll probably need a helper when it comes time to position them. Before moving the first post into position, drive stakes into the ground and nail a brace made from a 1 by 3 or 1 by 4 to each stake (use only one nail so the brace can pivot). Position the stakes far enough away from the end of the post so the braces can reach midway up the post when they are at a 45-degree angle, as shown at left.

Seat the post squarely in the anchor and

Right: Mark a straight cutoff line across the top of the post. Below: Using a combination square, carry the cutoff line all the way around the post.

check for plumb using a carpenter's level on adjacent sides. When the post is plumb, temporarily nail the braces to it.

Use a line level, laser level, or water level to mark the post at the proper height for the bottom of the rafters, according to your plans. If the structure is house-attached, this height is usually level with the bottom of the ledger. But pay particular attention to your design here, because rafter/ledger/beam connections vary. For example, if you are using a ledger that is wider than the rafters, you'll need to measure down from the ledger's top to determine where the bottom of the rafters will fall.

From that mark, subtract the actual thickness (or, in this case, the "height") of any beam that will sit between the post and

Set a power circular saw to cut at maximum depth, and then saw across the cutoff line, turn over the post, and cut from the other side.

rafters. Also subtract any necessary drop for roof pitch and, for a sloped rafter, the small notch in the rafter's underside where it rests on the beam (see page 72). Make a new mark and, using a combination square, continue it around the post's perimeter. This is your cutting line. Repeat for the remaining posts, and label each one so you know where to return it after cutting.

Cutting posts Set the blade of a circular saw to cut as deep as possible. For a 4-by-4 post, you will need to cut the post twice, on opposite sides. For a 6-by-6 post, cut along the line on all four sides and then finish the cut with a reciprocating saw or handsaw. Be sure to wear safety glasses, gloves, and a dust mask. Before permanently erecting the posts, seal the cut ends with a preservative and consider finishing them. If your design calls for metal post-and-beam connectors, attach them to the tops of the posts before raising the posts.

Seating heavy beams Hoisting a large beam atop a post over your head demands considerable strength; always get help for this stage of construction. After cutting it to the proper length, drag the beam into position next to the posts and slip a short length of 4 by 4 under one end. With a helper, raise that end of the beam and maneuver it into the post cap. Partially drive in one nail to secure the beam before you lift the other end. Raise the other end using the same technique. Then finish fastening the beam to the post caps.

Though metal post-and-beam connectors are strong and easy to use, you can secure this connection using other methods. For example, you can nail a pair of wooden cleats to each post's top. (See the opposite page for examples of both.) Or, for a design that utilizes paired 2-bys to provide the support a single beam would otherwise afford, you can mount pressure-treated plywood cleats to the underside of the pair and screw it to the post tops as shown in the project on page 92.

Bracing posts & beams Some codes require that certain post-and-beam designs have crossbracing for lateral stability during high winds or seismic events. Unless they have a steel or engineered structure, post-and-beam assemblies, particularly those for freestanding patio roofs, may require bracing for lateral stability. Roofs less than 12 feet high usually require bracing on the outside posts of the side not connected to the house.

The most common type of bracing, shown below right, is called Y bracing. Mark individual braces in position, and cut them on the ground. Nail them in place temporarily. Drill pilot holes for lag screws or bolts, and then permanently affix the braces.

Post-and-Beam Connections

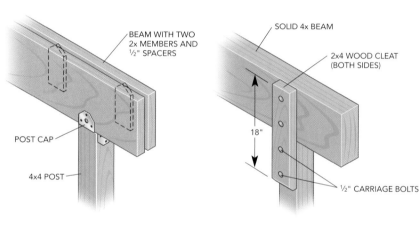

BEAM WITH TWO
2x MEMBERS AND
½" SPACERS

POST CAP

4x4 POST

SOLID 4x BEAM

2x4 WOOD CLEAT
(BOTH SIDES)

18"

½" CARRIAGE BOLTS

Y Bracing

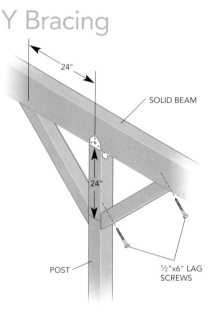

24"

SOLID BEAM

24"

POST

½"x6" LAG
SCREWS

Installing Rafters

Rafters spread roofing loads across beams, making it possible to use roofing materials too thin to span the distances between beams. Rafters must support their own weight over open space without sagging or twisting and also support the weight of the roof covering. For a roof that must shed water, they are sloped.

Rafter Construction

Rafters may connect to ledgers and beams any of several ways. The right method to use depends upon the roof's design.

Attaching rafters to a ledger With a house-attached overhead, rafters are fastened to the house at one end, as discussed on page 46. Metal framing connectors make the best connections. Joist hangers can hang rafters from a ledger, but notch the rafters or use special rafter hangers for sloping rafters. If rafters will sit on top of a ledger, attach them with seismic anchors as you would attach rafters to a beam.

Splicing rafters Where rafter connections will not be visible, rafters can be spliced together end-to-end with board lumber "gusset plates." To do this, butt the ends of the rafters together over a supporting beam. Then nail two pieces of 1-by or 2-by lumber

Building a gabled roof is a two-person job. Here, the first rafter is being marked for the bird's-mouth that will fit the top plate of the wall.

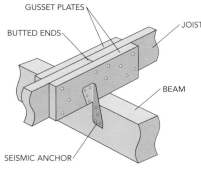

Rafters can be joined end-to-end as long as both rafters are supported by a beam. Two methods are shown here.

Use a framing square to mark the angled cut at the end of one rafter, and then use that rafter as a template for cutting the others.

of the same width as the rafters (see above left) and about 18 inches long centered over both sides of the splice. Or, join the members using manufactured metal splice plates.

Be sure each rafter end sits a full inch on the supporting beam. If you must splice several rafters, stagger the splices over different beams to prevent a weak substructure.

Another splicing method—though it does not utilize uniform spacing—is to overlap rafter ends supported by beams. If more than one splice is needed on a full rafter length, alternate overlapped sides.

For standard 2-inch lumber, nail both faces of each splice with six 8d or 10d common galvanized nails. This type of splicing, as shown in the illustration above, adds lateral stability to the rafters and may eliminate the need for bracing.

Detailing & Fastening Rafters

If you wish to add decorative detailing to rafters, do so before you lift and fasten them into place. Following are the methods for detailing, fastening, and bracing rafters.

Decorative rafter tails Decoratively cutting rafter ends can give a patio roof or

gazebo a distinctive style. You'll see many examples of decorative rafter-end treatments throughout this book. Use a saber saw for making curved cuts.

Sloping rafters Fitting sloped rafters in place can be tricky for a novice. It's usually easiest to cut one rafter to fit and then use it as a template for the rest, but this only works if the supporting beam and ledger (or second beam) are perfectly parallel.

To cut sloping rafters for a house-attached patio roof, first lay a rafter board so it rests on its edge on both the ledger and the beam parallel to the ledger. Then force the rafter's tip snugly against the house wall. Using a block of wood as a ruler, mark the ends for cutting. Cut the triangular piece off the rafter end

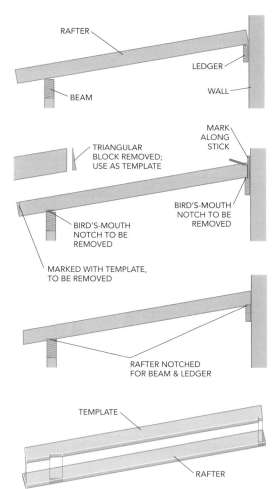

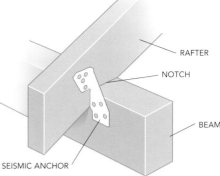

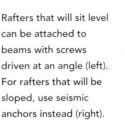

Rafters that will sit level can be attached to beams with screws driven at an angle (left). For rafters that will be sloped, use seismic anchors instead (right).

that rests on the ledger and off the end that rests on the beam, as shown on the opposite page. Cut notches where the rafter rests on the ledger and on the beam. Place the rafter in several positions along the ledger and the beam to check for fit. Then mark and cut the remaining rafters, using this rafter as a template. Before fastening the rafters in place, treat them with a wood finish.

Attaching rafters to beams There are various ways of attaching rafters to a beam. The most common method of fastening them to the top of a beam is to drive in screws at an angle, as shown above. When doing this, it may be necessary to drill pilot holes first so the wood doesn't split. If the rafters will slope, use seismic anchors (also known as rafter ties), as shown in the illustration at top right. Although one standard anchor is adequate in most cases, a second one may be required diagonally across from the first one in high-wind or seismic areas; consult your local building department for standards in your area. With conventional anchors, you must notch the rafters to fit or use a double-sided anchor to avoid notching.

Bracing rafters Where rafters span long distances or are spaced wide apart, they are prone to twist or buckle unless braced with blocking. The width of the rafters is also a consideration; those made from 2 by 8s or larger lumber require more blocking than those made from 2 by 6s. Spacing between

blocking is typically determined by local codes. If rafter spans are less than 8 feet, headers (perpendicular rafters) nailed across the rafter ends are adequate for rafters that sit on top of beams.

Snap a chalk line across the rafters where the blocking will go, and then work your way across the joists, measuring and notating the lengths of blocking you'll need to cut from the rafter material. Cut and code all the blocks to correspond to their locations.

The easiest method of placing the blocks is to stagger them from one side of the chalk line to the other, as shown in the illustration below. By using this technique, you'll be able to face-nail the blocks instead of toenailing them. Use 16d nails.

For a decorative accent and to hide metal post caps, you can cut and miter trim stock to fit around the post tops, as shown at right.

Trim stock, painted the same color as the rafters, will subtly cover metal post caps.

Bracing Rafters

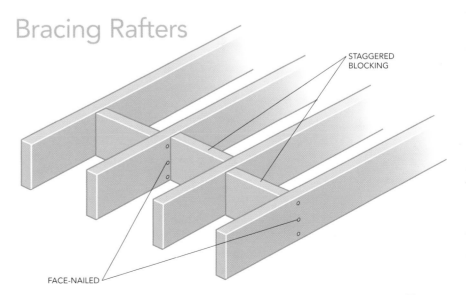

Roofing the Structure

Several different styles of roofing are used on patio overheads and gazebos, from open lattice-work to wood shingles. Installing open roofing such as lath or lattice panels is a relatively easy—though repetitive—job. Solid roof coverings intended to shed rain are more of a challenge, requiring a variety of basic roofing skills. Still others—glass, steel, built-up, and tile—are best left to professionals.

In this section you will find basic techniques for installing open-style roofing, asphalt shingles, and wood shingles. To make a decision about the most appropriate type of roofing for your structure, see the discussion of roofing characteristics on pages 23–26.

The illustrations below and opposite show several types of patio roofs and two methods of building a gazebo roof—one with open sheathing, the other with solid sheathing. The gazebo roof construction can just as easily be used on a patio roof.

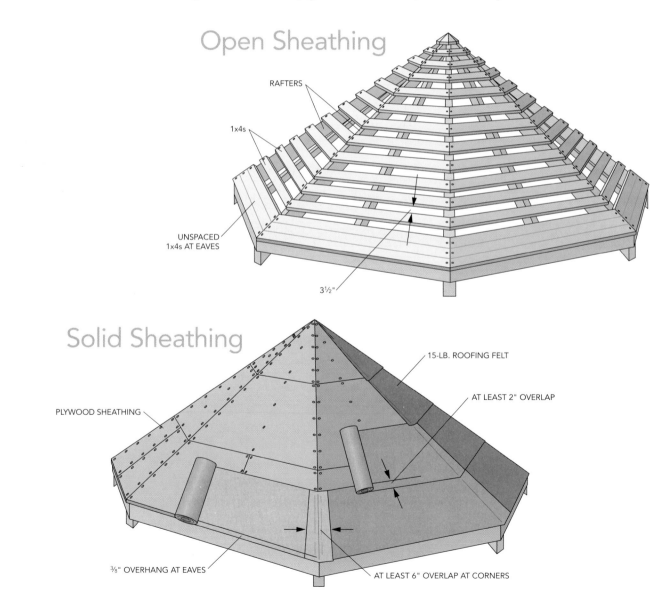

Open Sheathing

RAFTERS

1x4s

UNSPACED
1x4s AT EAVES

3½"

Solid Sheathing

PLYWOOD SHEATHING

15-LB. ROOFING FELT

AT LEAST 2" OVERLAP

⅜" OVERHANG AT EAVES

AT LEAST 6" OVERLAP AT CORNERS

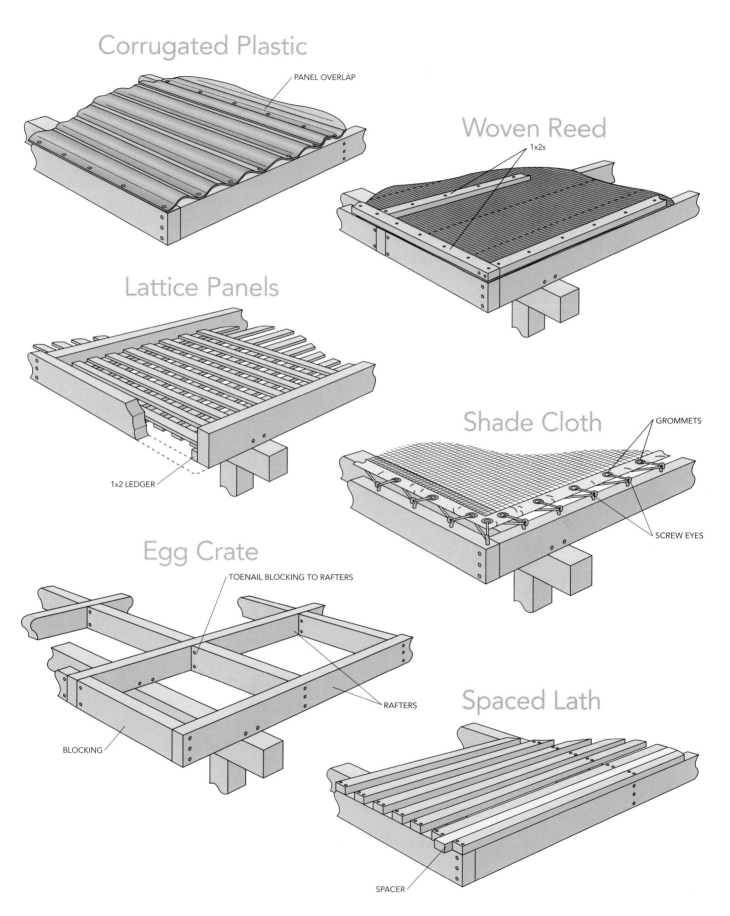

Corrugated Plastic

PANEL OVERLAP

Woven Reed

1x2s

Lattice Panels

1x2 LEDGER

Shade Cloth

GROMMETS

SCREW EYES

Egg Crate

TOENAIL BLOCKING TO RAFTERS

RAFTERS

BLOCKING

Spaced Lath

SPACER

Open-Style Roofing

Whether an open-style roof is made of thin latticework or substantial beams, construction techniques are similar. Some can even be built apart from the structure and then installed.

Lath, Battens & Boards

Whether you are using lath, battens, boards, or larger lumber, the width of the pieces and the spacing between them will determine the effect created by your overhead.

Creating shade Wood thickness and spacing can vary greatly—as can the amount of shade the variations create. For example, ⅜-inch lath laid flat and spaced 3 inches apart will not cast much shadow. But 2 by 2s spaced half an inch apart—or 1 by 3s on edge—will cast considerable shade.

Here are some spacing guidelines used by landscape architects: Space lath that is up to ½ inch thick ⅜ to ¾ inch apart. For stock that is ½ to 1⅛ inches thick, make the spacing between ¾ and 1 inch. You can space 2 by 2s up to 2 inches apart under certain circumstances, but spacing them 1 to 1½ inches will make the patio more comfortable in most cases.

The direction to run the roofing material depends on the time of day you want maximum shade. If you want the greatest relief from sun at noon, run the material east to west; if you want shade in the early morning and late afternoon, run it north to south.

It's a good idea to test your roofing material by temporarily nailing a small amount of it at various spacing intervals to the rafters so you can study the effects of each configuration at different times of the day. Keep in mind that the angle of the sun changes from season to season, not just during the course of a day.

Roof height will also affect the degree of light that falls on your patio or deck. The higher the roof, the more diffused the light becomes. The lower the roof, the sharper the shadows it will cast on the ground.

Suitable spans To prevent lattice-style roofing from sagging and warping, be conservative about the distances it spans. Do not span lath and batten more than 2 feet apart. You can span 1-bys up to 3 feet apart, but 2 feet is better; with 1-by-2-inch stock laid on edge—or with 2 by 2s—you can span 4 feet without objectionable sagging, but the boards may warp or curve a bit. Do not span any material more than 4 feet.

Sight down lumber to check for any crown (a curve along the edge); if the material has a crown, always face the convex side upward.

Nailing Before nailing any boards, double-check that they are spaced evenly and aligned perfectly. Set aside pieces that are overly twisted or bent. To keep the spacing consistent between closely spaced lattice or boards, cut a scrap of lumber to use as a spacer.

Always use galvanized or other corrosion-resistant nails to secure the wood to the framework. With ⅜- or ½-inch-thick lath, use 3d or 4d common or box nails. For use on 1-inch stock, choose 8d nails. Use 12d or 16d nails for thicker materials. Nail twice at

Lattice panels can be preassembled from 1 by 3s and fitted between rafters. Make each frame about ¼ inch narrower than the space, and rest the assembly on cleats.

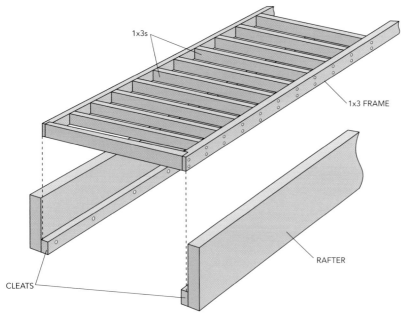

1x3s

1x3 FRAME

RAFTER

CLEATS

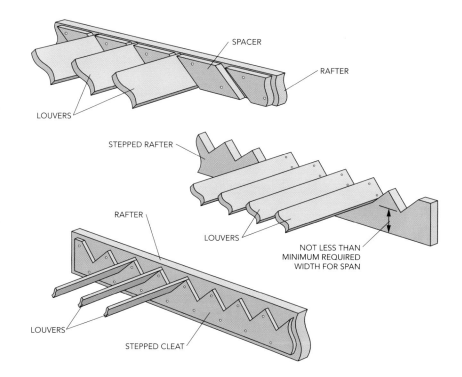

each rafter, and join cut ends directly over the rafters. If your wood tends to split, drill pilot holes before nailing.

Preassembly To reduce your time on the rooftop, preassemble panels and fasten them as shown in the illustration on the opposite page. You can make the panels practically any size, but 3 by 6 feet is the optimum dimension for lightweight material. Be sure the structural framing is true enough to receive the panels without a struggle.

Louvered Slat Roofing

Fixed louvers can be set at an angle to block the sun at the time of day it is most unwanted. Adjustable louvers can permit almost any degree of light or shade throughout the day.

Louver orientation Generally speaking, if you run louvers east to west, slanting the boards away from the sun, you will obstruct the midday sun and admit morning and afternoon sun. If you run them north to south, you will admit morning or afternoon sun, depending on the slant of the louvers.

Since a fixed-louver overhead is designed to block direct light for only part of the day, you will want to figure out what time the sun is highest in the sky during summer. When figuring louvers for a pitched roof, do not forget to factor in the angle of the pitch to the angle of the sun.

Installing fixed louvers Fixed louvers can be nailed directly to rafters, or they can be built in modular sections and then fastened in place. The illustrations at top right show three different ways of fastening louvers to their supports. If you cut stepped rafters, be sure that the width at the shallowest point is not less than that specified for the span.

For the louver material, 1 by 3s, 1 by 4s, or 1 by 6s not more than 3 feet long are best.

Installing adjustable louvers Though adjustable louvers can be exacting to build, they offer excellent sun control. If you do not want to attempt the precision work involved in making adjustable louvers, consider buying a ready-made system.

Shown below is one design for building your own system. Build the modules separately, and then fasten them between the rafters. Louvers should not exceed 4 feet in length; cut them slightly shorter than the space between the rafters. Use aluminum nails with the heads clipped off for the pins.

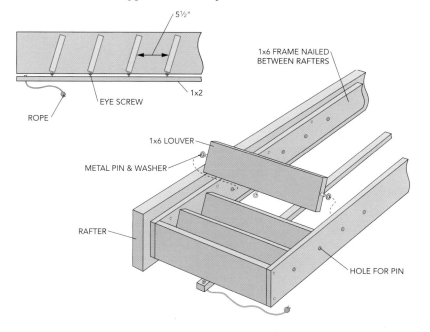

Solid Roofing

Do-it-yourselfers with moderate skills and an ability to work at heights can install many of the solid roofing materials used for houses on a patio overhead or gazebo. As with homes, asphalt shingles and wood shingles are by far the most popular. Before choosing a material, consider the pitch of your new structure's roof. In addition, you may have to apply underlayment and sheathing before you can install the roofing material.

Roof Pitch

The steeper a roof's pitch, the more likely it is that water will roll off without penetrating the material. "Pitch" refers to the vertical rise measured against a standard horizontal distance of 12 inches (see the photograph below). The term "4-in-12," applied to a roof, tells you that the roof rises 4 inches vertically for every 12 horizontal inches.

Asphalt shingles and wood shingles and shakes are designed for roofs with a 4-in-12 or greater slope. With additional underlayment, asphalt shingles can also be applied to 2-in-12 slopes and wood shingles and shakes to 3-in-12 slopes. (Do-it-yourself plastic and aluminum panels can be applied on slopes as gradual as 2 in 12—but they will not shed all water or bear the weight of snow.)

Building the Roof's Base

On house roofs, asphalt shingles are normally applied over plywood sheathing with an underlayment of 15-pound roofing felt.

Right: Attach fascia boards to the rafter tails.

To determine the pitch of a roof, first rest a carpenter's level on the roof so that it is level. Then, 12 inches from the end of the roof, measure straight down. This distance is how far the roof drops every 12 inches. In other words, if you find the measurement is 8 inches, then the roof has a pitch of 8-in-12.

Wood shingles are typically laid atop spaced 1-by-4 boards. Both constructions are illustrated by the gazebo roofs that are shown on page 75.

Adding fascia Once the rafters are in place, you can choose to add fascia, which covers the ends of the rafters to protect them

and provide a more finished look. A common fascia material is 1-by-4 or 1-by-6 primed pine. Cut the fascia boards to length, and attach them with two 8d galvanized nails driven into each rafter end. If two boards must be joined end-to-end, center the joint over a rafter.

Solid plywood sheathing Apply plywood sheathing over the rafters to serve as a sturdy nailing base. Although $\frac{1}{2}$- or $\frac{5}{8}$-inch sheathing is used on typical house roofs, most patio and gazebo roofs differ from house roofs in that, when they are viewed from below, do not have ceilings to hide the

Nail plywood sheathing to roof rafters, staggering the vertical joints so that they don't align. Next, roll out roofing felt and staple it in place, working from the eaves up.

construction. Therefore, thicker sheathing is preferred. In fact, you may want to choose a higher-grade material with a good side that can be faced downward and then painted or stained. Another option is to build a ceiling by nailing ⅜-inch plywood sheets to the undersides of the rafters.

Start at the bottom, and work your way to the top, making sure the end of each panel falls over the center of a rafter (leave ⅛ inch between edges and ¹⁄₁₆ inch between ends of adjoining panels to allow for expansion). Trim if needed. Stagger the vertical joints between plywood sheets—don't align them. Use 6d galvanized common or box nails for plywood that is up to an inch thick and 8d nails for plywood ⅝ inch or more. Space nails every 6 inches along the ends of each panel and every 12 inches at intermediate supports.

Flashing Flashing protects a roof at its most vulnerable points: where the roof connects to the structure, along eaves, in valleys, or anywhere water might seep into the sheathing. Flashing is most commonly made from malleable 28-gauge galvanized sheet metal. Plastic and aluminum flashing are available, as well. You can buy preformed flashing for drip edges and valleys or make your own. Use roofing nails to fasten it in place, positioning the flashing where roofing or adjoining flashing will cover it. Caulk any exposed nailheads.

Underlayment If you are using asphalt shingles, you will need to cover the decking

with roofing felt. To evenly align rows of roofing felt, measure the roof carefully and snap horizontal chalk lines before you begin. Be sure to snap the first line 33⅝ inches above the eaves (this allows for a ⅜-inch overhang). Then, providing for a 2-inch overlap between strips of felt, snap each succeeding chalk line at 34 inches.

When applying roofing felt, start at the eaves and roll the strips out horizontally along the roof, working toward the ridge or the top edge. Align the top edge with the chalk lines. The felt should be trimmed flush at the gable overhang and overlap 6 inches at any ridges, hips, or valleys. Wherever two strips meet in a vertical line, overlap them by 4 inches. Drive just enough roofing nails or staples to hold the felt in place until the roofing material is applied.

Adding a drip edge Before adding the asphalt shingles, protect the edges of the roof with drip-edge flashing. Drip edge is malleable metal that is preformed into a right angle with a slight lip along one edge to help direct water runoff away from the roof and exterior siding.

Installing spaced sheathing For wood shingles, install spaced sheathing. Lay 1-by-4 boards horizontally along the roof, using another 1 by 4 as a spacing guide. Fasten each board to the rafters with two 8d nails, allowing ⅛-inch spacing where boards meet. Start your installation with solid rows of 1 by 4s at the eaves and rakes.

Attach drip-edge flashing along the roof eaves. Tuck it under the roofing felt, and then nail it to the sheathing with roofing nails.

Applying Asphalt Shingles

Standard three-tab asphalt shingles are the easiest roofing material to install. They are a manageable weight and a breeze to cut and nail. In addition, the 12-by-36-inch shingles, when given a standard weather exposure of 5 inches, cover large areas very quickly.

Asphalt shingles should be applied over a solid deck of plywood sheathing with an underlayment of 15-pound roofing felt.

Installing asphalt shingles is a simple but repetitive process. First, apply an upside-down starter strip along the lower edge, and nail the first course on top of this. Then add additional courses, overlapping previous ones and staggering end joints. Finally, apply any hip or ridge shingles needed.

Cutting & nailing Cut asphalt shingles face down on a flat surface with a sharp utility knife. Hold a carpenter's square or straightedge on the cut line, and score the back of the shingle with the knife. Then bend the shingle back and forth to break it on the scored line.

Choose roofing nails that are short enough not to poke through the underside of the sheathing, typically 12-gauge galvanized roofing nails with $3/8$-inch-diameter heads. When nailing, drive the heads snug with the surface, and take special care to avoid breaking the shingle.

Laying shingles Asphalt shingles have a strip of self-sealing mastic that fastens them together once they are heated by the sun. In order for the first course of shingles to fasten to the front edge of the roof, begin by installing a special starter row. This row comprises 7-inch strips cut from full shingles and installed upside down along the eaves to position the mastic near the edge, where it will stick to the first full row installed.

Secure the starter row with roofing nails 3 inches above the eaves. Install the first course of shingles, allowing a $1/2$-inch overhang. Snap a chalk line 10 inches up from the bottom of the first course, and install the second course, offsetting it horizontally by a half tab. Continue snapping reference lines and adding courses until you reach the ridge.

At the ridge, use ready-made ridge shingles or cut your own 12-inch squares from standard shingles. On the most visible side of the structure, snap a line that is parallel to and 6 inches down from the ridge. Starting at one end, apply the shingles, leaving a 5-inch exposure; align the edges with the chalk marks. Nail on each side, $5^1/2$ inches from the butt and 1 inch from the outside edge.

Applying Wood Shingles

Wood shingles are installed with their tapered ends pointed up-roof on open sheathing, as shown at right. If the wood has a sawn side and a rough side, install the pieces with the rough side exposed. Correct exposure for wood shingles depends on both their length and the slope of the roof. The recommended exposures are shown in the chart below.

Nailing Use two rustproof nails per shingle. Choose 14½-gauge nails that have heads 7/32 inch wide and are 1¼ inches long (check the length to be sure that they will not poke through the sheathing's underside). Place a nail ¾ inch in from each side of a shingle, an inch above the butt line for the next course.

Trimming To make straight cuts along the grain of shingles, simply slice through them with a roofer's hatchet. When it is necessary to cut a shingle across the grain, use a utility knife to score it. If the wood is thin, break it against a hard edge. Otherwise, saw it.

Starter course & first course Combine the starter and first courses by laying the shingles one on top of the other. Note that shorter shingles are used for the starter course. Then overhang this double course 1½ inches at the eaves and rakes. Offset the joints between layers at least 1½ inches. Allow ¼ inch between shingles for the wood to expand and contract.

Successive courses When you lay the next courses, align the shingles both vertically and horizontally for proper exposure and coverage. You do not need to snap chalk lines for vertical alignment. Simply lay the random-width shingles according to this principle: Offset joints at least 1½ inches so that no joints in any three successive courses are in alignment.

To align the shingles horizontally, snap a chalk line at the proper exposure over the doubled starter/first course, or use your roofer's hatchet as an exposure guide. Then lay the lower edge of the next course on the chalk line and nail. Repeat in this manner, working your way up the roof until you reach the ridge or top.

At the ridge, let the last courses of shingles hang over, and then snap a chalk line above the center of the ridge board and trim all the ends at the same time. Cover the ridge with a strip of 30-pound roofing felt that is at least 8 inches wide.

Applying hip & ridge shingles Using factory-made ridge and hip shingles, double the starter courses at the bottom of each hip and at the end of the ridge, as shown at right. Exposure should not exceed the allowed weather exposure of the wood shingles on the roof planes. Start laying out the ridge shingles at the end of the ridge opposite the direction of prevailing winds. Use nails long enough (usually 2 to 2½ inches) to extend into the ridge board adequately.

Shingles are applied over spaced sheathing. With thick shakes, such as those shown above, interleaf each course with a layer of roofing paper.

Factory-made hip and ridge shingles protect the top edges of each roof plane. Overlap these shingles starting from the bottom up, just as you did with the main roof shingles.

Maximum Exposure for Wood Shingles

SIZE	3-IN-12 TO 4-IN-12 SLOPES	STEEPER SLOPES
16"	3¾"	5"
18"	4¼"	5½"
24"	5¾"	7½"

Note: Exposures are for No. 1 (Blue Label) quality.

How to Build a Gazebo

Though many of the principles and materials used for building patio roofs are also used in gazebo construction, gazebos are generally more complicated to build than patio roofs. For example, many gazebos have wooden floors, short walls, solid roofs, and considerable decorative detailing. In addition, their geometric shapes oftentimes require cutting compound angles, making difficult joints, and performing feats of carpentry that are beyond the skills of most do-it-yourselfers. In fact, even many accomplished carpenters often find building a non-rectangular or square gazebo to be a serious challenge.

The good news is that many quality woodworking companies produce gazebo kits that make the job much easier and more affordable than building a gazebo from scratch. With a gazebo kit, the manufacturer has done most of the cutting and joinery. The components are numbered or coded to correspond with accompanying diagrams and assembly directions. Some kits come in stacks of pre-cut pieces, others are partially panelized or preassembled by the manufacturer—in either case, assembly is a relatively easy

process. With these, you provide the site, build a simple foundation, put together the parts, and admire the results. In this section, we'll look at how to build a kit gazebo.

Kits also include screws, bolts, nails, and various connection brackets and plates. The best models use screws for all fastening, including flooring. When ordering, ask how soon your kit will be shipped and what to expect in shipping costs. Some companies will ship to you within 10 business days, and some offer free delivery within 50 miles. The distance from the manufacturer to your home can dramatically affect both the cost and the wait so it pays to explore regional and local makers first.

Many shapes, types, and styles of gazebos—made from a variety of materials—are available. You'll find octagonal, rectangular, and oval-shaped gazebos made from red cedar, treated pine, and even vinyl. Similarly, the roofs may be topped with any of several roofing materials, though cedar shakes are the most popular. Gazebo sizes can run from small 6-by-6-foot models to large 16-by-16-foot versions.

Red cedar gazebos Red cedar is a handsome material and, because of the natural oils in the wood, is resistant to decay and insect damage. The material of choice is often grade #1 Western red cedar. The roof of a cedar gazebo is usually covered with cedar shakes; the floor is also typically cedar. Basic models run from around $2,900 for a 6 by 6 to more than $7,000 for a 16 by 16.

A kit gazebo is built from precut, partly assembled components. Here, nearly all of the structural parts are in place.

Treated pine gazebos An option that is about 10 percent less expensive than an identically designed gazebo made of cedar is pine that has been pressure-treated with preservatives that prevent decay and insect infestation. Treated pine is meant to be stained or painted.

Vinyl gazebos Though vinyl is not intended to be a structural material, gazebos called "vinyl" have treated pine posts, braces, and rails that have been encapsulated with smooth, white PVC (vinyl). The resulting material is extremely durable and almost maintenance-free. Prices for standard designs with cedar shingle roofs and treated pine floors run from $3,300 for a 6 by 6 to $7,500 for a 16 by 16.

Gazebo options

When buying a kit, you can choose from a variety of options. These include screening inserts, acrylic or glass windows, deluxe braces, cupolas, electrical kits, and even swings. In addition, some companies offer custom modifications for price upgrades, including curved roofs, double roofs, lathe-turned spindles, and benches. Also check to see if the product can be purchased pre-stained with a protective sealer and/or a UV-protective stain. This option may cost from $600 to $700, but it can save you the effort of doing it yourself. If you choose to do the staining or painting, doing it prior to assembly will make the task much easier than standing atop a ladder and straining to reach into corners.

The techniques shown here will guide you through the basic principles of assembling a kit gazebo, but be sure to follow the manufacturer's directions of the model that you buy implicitly.

Because some of the components are heavy or awkward to handle, you will need a helper. In fact, you may want to employ two or three helpers when it comes time to lift the pre-assembled roof components into place. Also take note: Once you begin building the roof, you will be working with heavy materials at dangerous heights; if you are not comfortable with your qualifications for doing this type of work, call in a professional.

Construction

Before you begin assembly, you will need to prepare a foundation according to the manufacturer's directions. Though some kits are designed to sit on a concrete slab (see pages 66–67), most have wooden floors supported by a system of concrete piers. Proper layout of these foundation piers is crucial because the kit's components are sized to fit this layout. You will also need to check with your local building department to make sure the foundation meets local codes.

One easy and sure way to accurately lay out the foundation is to do a "dry run" with the floor's framing components. As illustrated in the photograph above, start by creating a level pad for the gazebo and then spreading about 4 inches of sand over the area's ground. Next, loosely assemble the floor's structural members. Once they are positioned, they will automatically indicate where the piers and posts must go. Mark their placements with stakes, and then remove the flooring components and dig holes for the footings and piers. (For more about pouring footings and placing piers, see pages 65–66.)

To identify the placement of piers and posts, loosely assemble flooring components where the gazebo will stand.

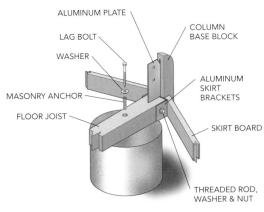

With this kit, triangular floor units are supported by rectangular footings. The gazebo's posts are attached at each corner.

Floor framing The proper method for building the floor framing depends on the kit you buy. The kit shown in the photograph above utilizes triangular structural floor units that sit on rectangular footings and support the gazebo's vertical posts. The alternate method shown in the illustrations below has floor joists that radiate out from a central hub; the gazebo's posts connect to special column base blocks, as shown in the detail at top right. With either style, you begin by fastening the structural members to the foundation pier at the center. The octagon's points should be in line with the outer piers. But before you begin to fasten the joists to the outer piers, site down each joist to make sure that its end lines up straight with the end of the opposite joist.

Floor sections If your kit has individual joists, the next step is to connect the ends of each joist with skirt boards. For the kit shown in the illustration below, you make each connection with a threaded rod, washers and nuts, aluminum skirt brackets, and column base blocks. Be sure the skirt boards' top edges sit flush with the top of the floor joists. Finger-tighten a nut (with washer) at each end of each threaded rod. Then, tighten the nuts at the center plate, and, using lag screws, bolt the floor joists to anchors in the concrete piers.

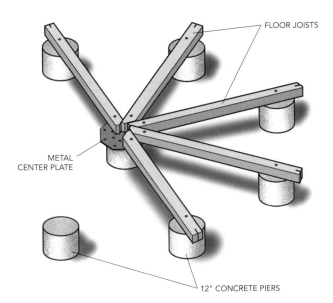

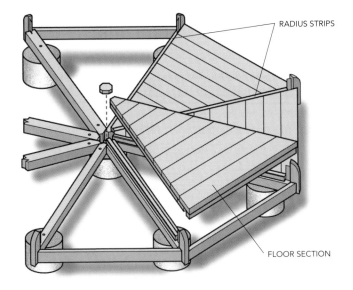

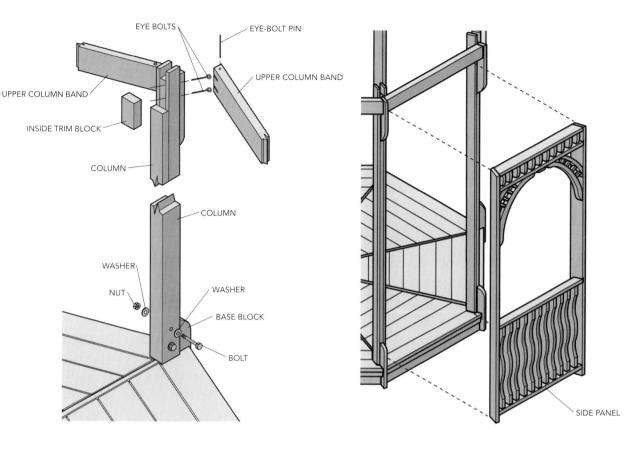

EYE BOLTS

EYE-BOLT PIN

UPPER COLUMN BAND

UPPER COLUMN BAND

INSIDE TRIM BLOCK

COLUMN

COLUMN

WASHER

WASHER

NUT

BASE BLOCK

BOLT

SIDE PANEL

To install the floor sections, line up each section's edges with the centerlines of the floor joists. If necessary, use a mallet to gently tap the floor sections toward the center until they are tightly together and the outer edges of the floor nailers are even. Then use galvanized screws to fasten the floor sections to the joists.

Columns If your kit's columns are not an integral part of the floor system, the next step is to bolt them to the base blocks. Then assemble the upper column bands at the top of the columns. Just finger-tighten the nuts until all of the upper column bands are placed. Tighten the nuts, alternating between the right and left nuts on each column. Screw the inside trim blocks in place with 3-inch trim screws.

Side panels Install the side panels by positioning each panel so it has equal margins on each side, and then attach each panel

to the columns, typically with 2½-inch screws. Preassembled side panels are heavy and a bit awkward to maneuver, so be sure to have a helper on hand. You will also need a couple of tall stepladders.

Preassembled side panels include secondary posts, rails, balusters, headers, and other decorative components.

Assemble a pair of rafters with the central hub flat on the ground, and then stand them up next to the structure, as shown at right. With helpers, position and secure the truss at the tops of two opposing posts, as shown below (but beware—this assembly won't be stable yet). Secure each additional rafter.

Roof framing Once all of the side panels are in place, it's time for the most difficult part of assembly—placing the rafters. Start by laying opposing rafters on a flat, level surface and screwing them to the central hub. With at least one helper (you may need two or three), fit the ends of this truss onto a pair of opposing posts. Be sure the bird's-mouth cuts at the rafter ends seat fully. Then screw the rafters to the post tops. With one person on a ladder near the center, position and screw the remaining rafters in place.

Some models, such as the gazebo shown in the photographs on these two pages, employ horizontal blocking between the rafters. Once all of the rafters are in position, fit and screw this blocking in place, working from the bottom tier upward.

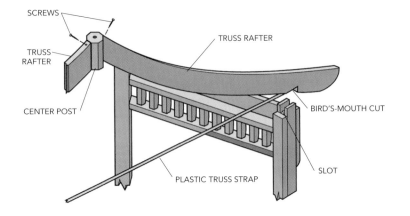

SCREWS

TRUSS RAFTER

TRUSS RAFTER

CENTER POST

BIRD'S-MOUTH CUT

PLASTIC TRUSS STRAP

SLOT

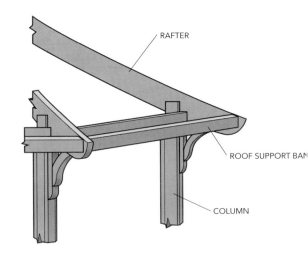

RAFTER

ROOF SUPPORT BA

COLUMN

For a large, 15-foot gazebo, it may be necessary to install a roof support band or, for a screened model, a screen band around the perimeter. Being sure to keep the band flush with the top edge of the rafters, screw it in place. Next, install the eaves band, positioned a uniform distance from the rafter ends.

Roof sections Next comes the really heavy lifting. Lean three long boards against the roof support band to serve as a ramp for sliding the first roof section up into place, as shown in the photograph above. Position yourself on a ladder at the edge of the rafter and have a helper lift and slide the section into place (this may take two helpers and/or you may need to climb up onto the roof framing and help pull the section up). Center the section's edges over the rafters. Screw it in place with 3-inch screws through predrilled holes. Repeat this process with the other sections.

Place the peak cap on top so that its threaded rod is projecting up through the cap's center, and then screw down the finial, securing it against the peak cap. If you are installing a small cupola on top, use a longer threaded rod and place the cupola's body between the roof and the peak cap.

The gazebo shown utilizes special banding to cover the gaps between the roof sections. Install this according to the directions.

Finishing Install the trim pieces, including the handrails. Set any exposed nailheads beneath the surface and fill the holes with matching wood filler. If you have stained or painted the structure's pieces prior to assembly, touch them up now.

Roof sections are easiest to handle if you slide them up a ramp made from long boards (top left). One person can pull from the top as the other lifts and pushes the section up (top right). Cover seams between the roof sections with banding made for this job (above).

Handrails and other finishing touches come last. Use glue, clamps, and finishing nails to attach highly visible members. Set the nailheads, fill with wood filler, sand, and finish.

Finishing Wood Parts

Most wood for outdoor use needs a finish to preserve its beauty and protect it from decay. Whether you choose a water repellent, a semitransparent or solid-color stain, or paint, test it on a sample board first to make sure you like the way it looks. Be sure to follow label directions carefully and allow the finish to dry thoroughly before making your judgment.

Though finishing your structure before you have built it may seem like the furthest thing from your mind, it is much easier to finish some or most of the material at ground level. You just need to set up a pair of sawhorses to support the wood.

Water repellents (water sealers) help keep wood from warping and cracking. They may be clear or slightly tinted; the clear sorts do not color the wood but let it fade gradually to gray. You can buy either oil- or water-based

are essentially thin paints that cover the wood grain completely. For custom tints, you can usually mix any paint color you choose into this base.

Paints cover wood completely and come in an array of colors. Because they hide defects so thoroughly, they allow you to use lower grades of lumber where strength is not a consideration. Most painters recommend using a two-step procedure for outdoor structures: First, apply an alkyd- or oil-based prime coat,

From left to right: Unfinished redwood, clear water sealer, tinted oil-based repellent, gray semitransparent stain, and red solid-color stain.

products, many of which include UV blockers and mildewcides. Do not use clear-surface finishes such as spar varnish or polyurethane on outdoor lumber. In addition to being costly, they wear quickly and are very difficult to renew.

Available in both water- and oil-based versions, semitransparent stains contain enough pigment to tint the wood's surface with just one coat while still letting the natural grain show through. You will find grays and wood tones as well as products to "revive" an unpainted structure's natural wood color or dress up pressure-treated wood.

To cover a structure in a solid color, you can choose either opaque stain or paint. Stains for siding, decking, and similar areas

and then follow it with one or two topcoats of water-based (latex) enamel. Ideally, the primer should cover all surfaces of the lumber (including the inner faces of built-up posts, beams, and rafters), so if you choose to paint, you definitely want to prime before assembly. You can apply topcoats after the structure is completed, or apply topcoats before assembly and touch up afterward.

Heavy-bodied stains may be brushed or sprayed on; paint can be applied with a brush, roller, or spray gun. A favored technique for painting lumber is to roll on the paint and then brush it into the wood with a 2- or 4-inch paintbrush, depending upon the size of the stock. It's easiest to spray complex components such as lath and lattice.

Wiring an Outdoor Shelter

Electrical amenities can greatly increase the comfort and functionality of a gazebo or other outdoor shelter. Lighting is an obvious must for nighttime activities. A ceiling fan can stir up the breezes in an enclosed gazebo or patio room, and electrical outlets offer a place to plug in a laptop computer or music system.

Here we look at how to install and wire electrical devices. For more complex wiring, or if you don't feel adept at working safely with electricity, call an electrician.

Keep in mind that if outdoor lighting is all you want, you can buy a low-voltage outdoor lighting system, which is far easier and safer to install yourself than is a standard-voltage system. Installation instructions for all low-voltage systems are included in the kit.

The instructions given here for standard-voltage wiring assume an electrical circuit is nearby and that you can safely extend this circuit to handle the additional load of the lights, fan, and any receptacles you may be adding to your outdoor structure.

Ask your local building department if there are any necessary permits, inspections, or restrictions. Before beginning work on any wiring, shut off the power to the circuit you will be connecting to by removing the fuse or switching off the circuit breaker. Then, tape the circuit breaker in the OFF position, or lock the service panel.

Materials

Because outdoor wiring must withstand the elements, outdoor electrical materials are stronger and more resistant to corrosion than those used for indoor wiring. Also, because outdoor components must fit together tightly to prevent water from seeping into them, heavy-duty gaskets or special fittings often seal cover plates on outdoor electrical boxes.

An outdoor receptacle fits in a watertight housing box. These boxes are made of cast aluminum, zinc-dipped iron, or bronze and have threaded entries to keep out water. All covers for watertight boxes are sealed with gaskets, and many switch boxes are equipped with an exterior on/off lever that enables you to operate the switch without having to open the cover.

To prevent accidental shock, codes specify that any new outside receptacle be protected with a ground-fault circuit interrupter (GFCI). A GFCI circuit breaker may be installed in the service panel to protect the

WATERTIGHT FIXTURE BOX

WATERTIGHT SWITCH BOX

EXTENDER RING

GASKET

COVER PLATE

"WHILE-IN-USE" COVER

EXTERIOR SWITCH PLATE

LAMP SOCKET

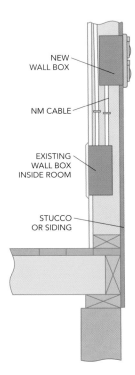

NEW
WALL BOX

NM CABLE

EXISTING
WALL BOX
INSIDE ROOM

STUCCO
OR SIDING

entire circuit, or a GFCI receptacle may be installed. The latter method is less expensive in most cases; the receptacle is protected, as are any other receptacles installed in the circuit from that point onward (commonly referred to as "downstream").

A fan should only be installed beneath a solid roof that reliably sheds water. Be sure to choose a "damp-rated" model that will survive the moist conditions of an outdoor room. If the unit will be exposed to corrosive coastal air or particularly moist conditions, choose a "wet-rated" fan.

Electrical codes may allow you to run type UF cable with two No. 12 conductors and a ground conductor to the structure. You can usually bury the cable in the ground, but, where it would be exposed or subject to damage, run it through a ¾-inch-diameter conduit.

Rigid, nonmetallic (PVC schedule 40) conduit is the most popular type for outdoor use where codes permit it, and it is the best choice for direct burial because it is lightweight and does not corrode. PVC conduit comes in 10-foot lengths, each with one coupling for joining it to additional lengths. Other fittings are available for configuring runs, including 90-degree angles and condulets that allow for a T connection.

Special PVC housing boxes are designed for use with plastic conduit (they are different than the plastic electrical boxes used for indoor electrical cable). Be aware that non-metallic conduit does not constitute a grounded system; you must run a separate grounding wire or use cable that includes a separate ground conductor.

Connecting to a Circuit

The easiest way to tap into an existing circuit is to install a new receptacle or junction box back-to-back with an existing box in an interior room, as shown at left. Alternatively, you can have an electrician run one or more dedicated circuits for outdoor use, routing cable from the service entrance panel or sub-panel to a drip-tight subpanel outdoors. You must utilize exposed conduit or buried UF cable outside.

Installing Conduit & Cable

Cutting lengths of PVC conduit and joining them together with fittings is easy work. You can cut PVC conduit with a hacksaw, hand-saw, or pipe cutter. After cutting, trim the ends inside and out with a pocketknife to remove any rough edges. Glue conduit and fittings together with gray conduit cement (not the water pipe cement used with PVC irrigation pipe).

Fasten the conduit and boxes to the structure's support members within 4 feet of each box or fitting. Push the wire or cable through the conduit (for long runs of conduit, you may have to rent or buy a "fish tape" to draw the wire through the conduit).

Simply screw a ceiling box to a joist or an exposed beam. Position the box so it will hide the hole drilled for the cable. Do not make cable or wire splices in this type of box; it's big enough to accommodate only two conductors and a grounding wire.

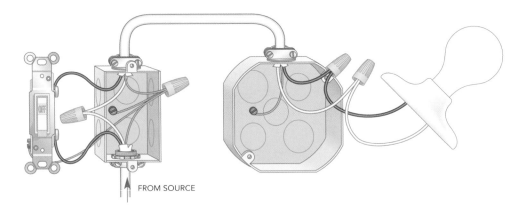

FROM SOURCE

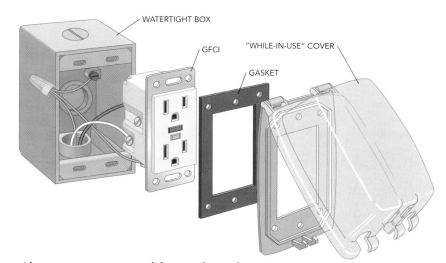

Wiring a Light

For standard-voltage lighting, you will need to install electrical boxes for the fixture and switch and wire them as shown below left. Be sure to use watertight outdoor housing boxes unless they are sheltered. The simplest ceiling box to use in a room protected by a roof is a low-profile "pancake" box, which you can screw to a beam or rafter (first remove the center knock-out). Position it so it will hide a hole drilled for the cable. Don't make wire or cable splices in this type of box; it's big enough to accommodate only two conductors and a grounding wire.

Wiring a Receptacle

Wire a receptacle as shown above right. When wiring a receptacle, use a wire nut to connect the ground wires to the receptacle's ground and the electrical box's green screw (if it has one). Connect the white wire to the silver terminal or white wire on the receptacle and the black wire to the brass terminal or black wire. Finish installation and affix the cover plates before turning the power back on.

Installing a Ceiling Fan

A ceiling fan requires at least 7 feet of clearance between the fan blades and the floor. For an area that is smaller than 225 square feet, buy a 42- or 44-inch fan. For larger spaces, you may want a 52-inch fan.

Most ceiling fans can easily be substituted for an existing overhead light fixture; the wall switch controls the fixture. Alternatively, you can buy a fan that comes equipped with a remote control system.

One person can install a ceiling fan. However, the motor weighs approximately 40 pounds, so you may wish to have a helper handy once it's time to lift the heavy components into place.

Before beginning work, be sure to turn off power to the circuit at the service panel.

Always use an approved box and attachment that is specified by the fan manufacturer. In general, a fan must hang from a hanger bracket that is fastened to a metal junction box. The box must be securely bolted to the structural members above. If the ceiling angles upward, the open side of the hanger bracket should face the high side.

You can assemble most of the pieces on site. Assemble the fan's downrod motor unit, and then fasten and tighten the downrod in the unit's collar. Slide the collar, canopy, and ball onto the downrod, running the wires out the top of the ball. A pin that passes horizontally through the top of the downrod holds the ball in place. After pushing the pin through the holes in the downrod, pull the ball up over the pin and secure it with its set screw. Lift the assembly up, and slide the ball into the hanger bracket. Rotate the assembly until the ball locks.

Twist and connect the wires with wire nuts, according to the manufacturer's directions. In most cases, you will be connecting the fan's green wire to the box's bare (grounding) wire, the fan's white wire to the box's white (neutral) wire, and the fan motor's black and blue wires to the box's black (hot) wire. Carefully push the connected wires up into the box and screw the canopy in place. Last, add the radio receiver to the bottom of the fan for the remote control, and secure the fan blades to the motor unit.

Designed to complement the house's architecture, this shade structure has crisp, rectilinear lines yet just enough detail—an ogee profile cut into the rafter and beam ends—to give it a classic look. Though the structure stands directly next to the house, it is completely self-supporting. Design: Wendy Walker

Design Details

The shade structure's easy-to-build design utilizes several different sizes of lumber, including 8-by-8 posts, 2-by-8 crossbeams, 2-by-6 rafters, and 1-by-2 lattice. Note that the 1-by-2 lattice is spaced 21½ inches apart from center to center to permit more sunlight than create shade. For a cooler, shadier patio, lay out the lattice on 6-inch centers.

To give the unit lateral strength, and to hold the posts erect during construction, galvanized pipes run from the concrete footings up into a deep hole drilled into the center of each post's bottom. You will need a ½-inch power drill and an extra-long 1⅛-inch auger or spade bit for drilling the posts; if you don't own these tools, you can rent them. Alternatively, instead of a 20-inch (or longer) drill bit, you can use a shorter bit with an extension shaft.

If you are building the structure over an existing patio, attach the posts with metal post anchors, bolting the anchors to the concrete slab as discussed on page 60.

For cutting the curved ogee profiles at the ends of the beams and rafters, use a saber saw with an extra-long blade or use a portable band saw.

Building Notes

All of the structure's members, with the exception of the posts, were painted before assembly. If your foundation layout is precise, you should be able to accurately precut all of the pieces before assembly. After you cut the pieces to size, apply a coat of primer and two topcoats of paint. Prime and paint the posts after assembly is complete, and touch up the rest of the structure.

Step-By-Step

1 Lay out and pour the footings according to the plan shown below and as discussed on page 65. While the concrete is still plastic, insert a 42-inch length of ¾-inch galvanized pipe vertically in each footing, leaving 18 inches of the pipe protruding from the top.

2 Use a ½-inch drill equipped with a long 1⅛-inch auger bit to drill a 19-inch-deep hole into a post bottom. Center the hole, and drill it as straight as possible. Repeat with the other five posts.

Patio Shade Structure Materials Checklist

- Concrete & #4 rebar for footings
- 8x8 posts
- 2x8 crossbeams
- 2x6 rafters
- 1x3 trim
- 1x2 lattice strips
- ½-inch pressure-treated plywood
- ¾-inch galvanized pipe
- Galvanized nails
- Deck screws
- Wood preservative, primer & paint
- Sanding & finishing supplies

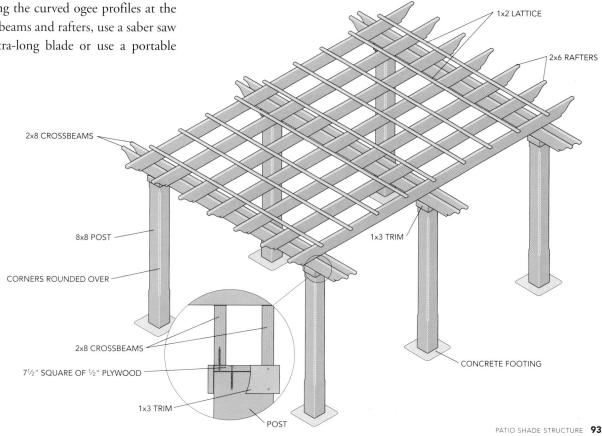

1x2 LATTICE

2x6 RAFTERS

2x8 CROSSBEAMS

8x8 POST

CORNERS ROUNDED OVER

2x8 CROSSBEAMS

7½" SQUARE OF ½" PLYWOOD

1x3 TRIM

POST

1x3 TRIM

CONCRETE FOOTING

Plan View

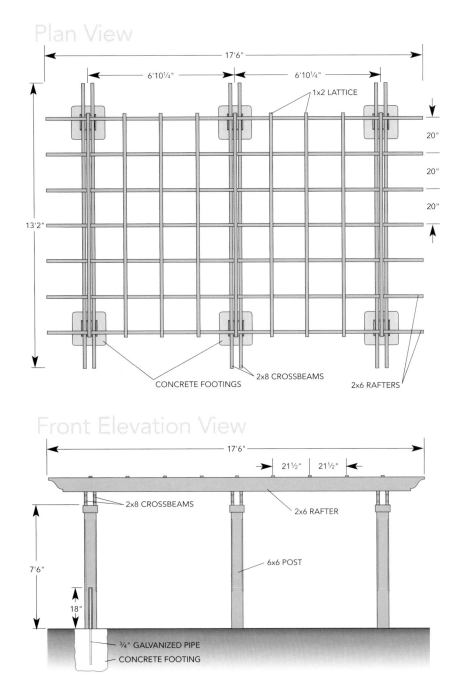

17'6"

6'10¼"   6'10¼"

1x2 LATTICE

20"

20"

20"

13'2"

CONCRETE FOOTINGS

2x8 CROSSBEAMS

2x6 RAFTERS

Front Elevation View

17'6"

21½" 21½"

2x8 CROSSBEAMS

2x6 RAFTER

6x6 POST

7'6"

18"

¾" GALVANIZED PIPE

CONCRETE FOOTING

3 Soak the bottom of each post with preservative, and then, with the aid of a helper, lift each post over a pipe and slide it down onto the footing as shown in the photograph at the top of page 66. Repeat with the remaining five posts. Use a level to check each post for plumb, as discussed on page 69. Make slight adjustments by driving cedar shims beneath the posts.

4 Assemble three sets of doubled 2-by-8 beams, and then fasten them together with 7½-inch squares of ½-inch pressure-treated plywood, as shown below left. Drive three galvanized deck screws into the bottom of each 2 by 8.

5 Align one of the assembled beams with two posts. With a helper, lift the beam onto the posts, and screw the plywood squares to the post tops, securing each with five deck screws, as shown in the photograph below right. Repeat with the other two beams.

6 Mark the positions of the seven 2-by-6 rafters on top of the beams—they are spaced 20 inches from center to center. Then, with your helper, set the rafters up on the beams near their final positions.

7 Roll each rafter up into position on its marks, and secure it to the beams, driving 3-inch deck screws at an angle from both sides (see the photograph at top on page 73). If the wood tends to split, drill pilot holes for the screws.

8 Mark the positions of the nine 1-by-2 lattice strips on top of the 2-by-6 rafters, 21½ inches from center to center. Use a chalk line to snap lines for the placement of the 1 by 2s across the rafters. Place each 1 by 2 so that it overlaps the first rafter by 2 inches, and then fasten it with a 2-inch deck screw, as shown in the photograph at right.

9 Use galvanized finishing nails to fasten mitered 1-by-3 trim around each post top to conceal the plywood plates and create a

decorative accent (see the photograph at right on page 73). Then, using a router equipped with a ¾-inch chamfering bit, cut a chamfer along the four corners of each post. For the posts shown, the cuts were stopped 20 inches above ground level and 3 inches from the top trim. Make several passes with your router, cutting progressively deeper to prevent the wood from splitting.

10 Sand the chamfers, and then prime and paint the posts.

Shade Arcade

Casting partial shade on the house and defining the path, this overhead illustrates how a patio roof can integrate a house with such landscaping elements as walkways, lawns, and planting beds. The structure features an arcade that nestles up against the house and then widens to encompass the garden and an entertainment patio.

Short connector posts, beveled at top and bottom, join perpendicular beams yet do not interfere with sight lines. Open-style roofing is made from 2 by 3s turned on edge and spaced on 6-inch centers. The surface lumber is painted.

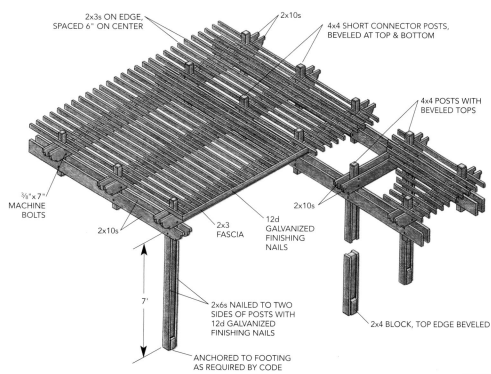

2x3s ON EDGE, SPACED 6" ON CENTER

2x10s

4x4 SHORT CONNECTOR POSTS, BEVELED AT TOP & BOTTOM

4x4 POSTS WITH BEVELED TOPS

⅜" x 7" MACHINE BOLTS

2x10s

2x3 FASCIA

12d GALVANIZED FINISHING NAILS

2x10s

7'

2x6s NAILED TO TWO SIDES OF POSTS WITH 12d GALVANIZED FINISHING NAILS

2x4 BLOCK, TOP EDGE BEVELED

ANCHORED TO FOOTING AS REQUIRED BY CODE

Project | Hillside Gazebo

Perched on the edge of a hillside, this redwood gazebo is accessed by a bridge from a formal garden with a fountain. The trellis roof filters sunlight to the structure's 100-square-foot interior. Landscape architect: R.M. Bradshaw & Associates

Design Details

Because it is located on a steep hillside, this gazebo captures outdoor living space that otherwise would have been unusable. Redwood planks laid in an octagonal pattern form the flooring, mirroring the shape of the roof for a finishing touch. The decorative facade between the posts just below the roof beams helps to anchor the roof, contributes to the overall sense of shelter and privacy, and serves to support flowering, climbing vines. A copper-clad cupola hiding the steel central hub ring is a focal point.

The relatively wide spacing of the 2-by-2 lattice (6 inches on center) is suitable for mild climates. This wide spacing was also chosen because it is visually interesting when viewed from above—the home's main living area is on the second floor overlooking the garden. Simply tightening the spacing will create more shade for hot climates.

Building Notes

Perhaps the single most important step in building a gazebo is making sure the post anchors are precisely positioned. Doing so requires maintaining a careful layout, bracing the anchors until the concrete sets up, and, if need be, shaving a post or two to adjust their positions.

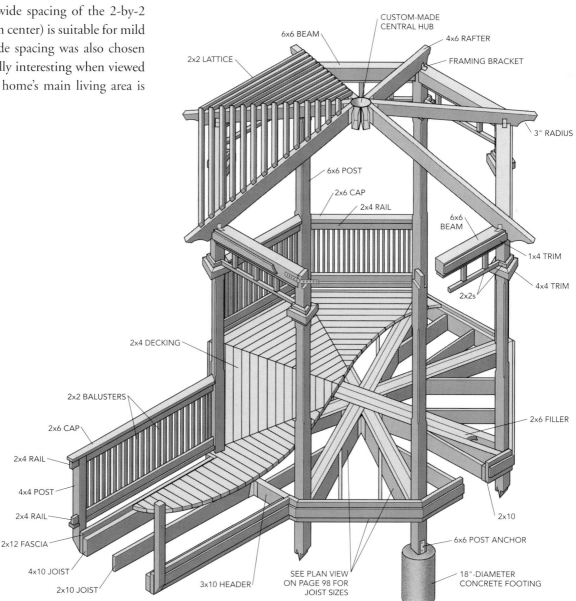

Framing brackets—either those designed to be bent to a desired angle or those already formed in angles typically encountered when framing an octagonal shape—are easier to use than fasteners alone and provide a stronger connection. Galvanized screws and bolts are used throughout.

Decking is spaced according to the lumber species used—in the case of redwood, about ¼ inch apart—to allow for expansion due to the elements. The floor structure, which is not visible, is framed with Douglas fir, a species that is prized for its strength and is also less costly than redwood. Sheet-metal straps, especially important in earthquake regions, tie the floor system together.

Step-By-Step

1 Make forms, and pour eight 18-inch-diameter concrete pier footings. Embed 6-by-6 post anchors into the wet concrete, and brace them in position until the concrete cures.

2 While the concrete is curing, measure and cut the posts. Notch the tops to create shoulders for the beams to rest on, and, using a router, mill a ¾-inch radius at each post corner. Sand the posts using 120-grit paper and then install them.

3 Lay the floor next, securing each pair of radiating joists to the sides of the posts with machine bolts. Screw sheet-metal straps onto the first layer of the perimeter joists to tie the corners together. Add 2-by-6 fillers between paired joists. Install the 2-by-4 decking with exterior screws.

4 Cut the beams to identical lengths, and miter the ends. Next, position the beams, and attach them to the posts with screws driven in at an angle. Screw two sheet-metal straps into the faces of the beams to tie them at the posts.

Elevation View

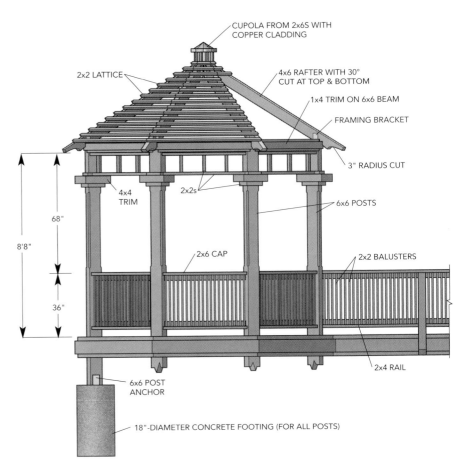

CUPOLA FROM 2x6S WITH COPPER CLADDING

2x2 LATTICE

4x6 RAFTER WITH 30° CUT AT TOP & BOTTOM

1x4 TRIM ON 6x6 BEAM

FRAMING BRACKET

3" RADIUS CUT

4x4 TRIM

2x2s

6x6 POSTS

2x6 CAP

2x2 BALUSTERS

68"

8'8"

36"

2x4 RAIL

6x6 POST ANCHOR

18"-DIAMETER CONCRETE FOOTING (FOR ALL POSTS)

Plan View of Floor

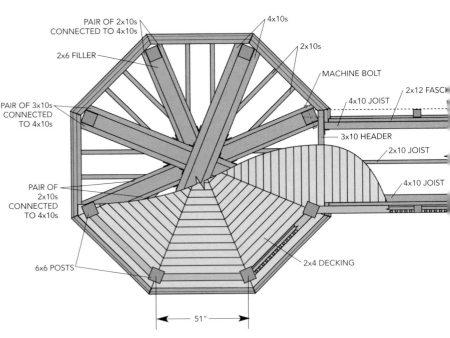

PAIR OF 2x10s CONNECTED TO 4x10s

4x10s

2x6 FILLER

2x10s

MACHINE BOLT

2x12 FASCIA

4x10 JOIST

PAIR OF 3x10s CONNECTED TO 4x10s

3x10 HEADER

2x10 JOIST

PAIR OF 2x10s CONNECTED TO 4x10s

4x10 JOIST

6x6 POSTS

2x4 DECKING

51"

5 Lay out the rafters, cut them to length, and then cut 30-degree angles at both ends. Cut a 3-inch radius on the tails using a jigsaw or band saw. Test them for fit, and then sand all the pieces using 120-grit paper. Install them using framing brackets at the beams and hangers welded to the central hub.

6 First, trace the central hub's outside dimension onto a 2-by wood block so the cupola can be built and clad offsite. Tack the mitered posts to the template wood, centering them on each of the eight sides. Cut the roof planes from 2-by-6 stock, and then glue and screw them all together. Copper-clad the top. Attach the posts to the underside of the roof with screws driven in at an angle. Remove the template, and install the cupola with screws driven through the posts into the rafters.

7 Sand the 2-by-2 lattice with 120-grit paper, and then cut it. Starting at the cupola, mark the lattice layout 6 inches on center on the tops of the rafters. Install the lattice with exterior screws. To keep from splitting or splintering the 2 by 2s, bore pilot holes and countersink the screws.

8 Install the 1-by-4 trim on the outside face of the beams to conceal the metal strapping. Cut and assemble the 2-by-2 components for the decorative facade under the beams, and then install the pieces with galvanized finishing nails. Install the mitered 4-by-4 and 2-by-2 capital trim that runs around the posts below the facade.

9 Sand all of the wood members using 120-grit paper. Cut and assemble each railing section by attaching 2-by-2 balusters to the wide faces of 2-by-4 rails cut to rough length. Make the final cuts so the spacing between the end balusters and the posts will be equal. Cut and install the bottom flat rail, install the baluster assembly, and, finally, mill, cut, and install the 2-by-6 cap.

10 When construction is complete, check to make sure all the fasteners are flush with or set just slightly below the surface, and then do a final sanding, especially on any areas within easy reach or that are close to view. Finally, apply a protective finish such as a semitransparent stain to minimize the effects of weathering.

Hillside Gazebo Materials Checklist

- Concrete, #4 rebar & form lumber for footings
- 6x6 posts & beams
- 2x6 fillers & cupola stock
- 2x10 joists
- 2x12 fascia
- 3x10 joists & headers
- 4x10 joists
- Custom-fabricated steel central hub
- 2x4 decking
- 4x6 rafters
- 2x2 trellis stock
- 1x4, 2x2 & 4x4 trim
- 2x2, 2x4 & 2x6 railing members
- Galvanized nails & outdoor screws
- Galvanized machine bolts, washers & nuts
- Expansion anchors
- Metal post anchors
- Metal framing brackets & fasteners
- Copper finial, flashing & nails
- Sheet-metal straps
- Sanding & finishing supplies
- Paint, stain, or wood preservative

Plan View of Roof

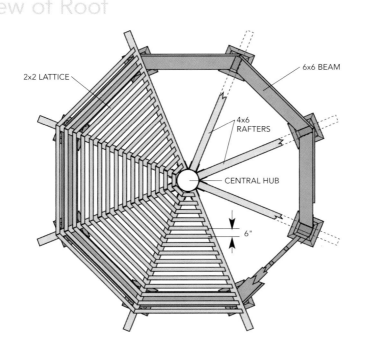

2x2 LATTICE

6x6 BEAM

4x6 RAFTERS

CENTRAL HUB

6"

Customized Kit Gazebo

The handsome gazebo featured on this book's cover appears to be custom-designed but is actually made from a gazebo kit. Rather than order all stock components from the kit manufacturer, the designers specified a few special touches. Some of these were taken care of by the manufacturer—most notably the custom X-panel railings. Others were handled on site: A roofing contractor applied handsome fiber-cement roofing shingles, and a masonry contractor built a concrete floor with a stone surface.

The gazebo is built from kiln-dried clear redwood. Posts, rails, braces, and all other components were precut, notched, and tooled by the manufacturer. Even the easy-to-assemble, pie-shaped tongue-and-groove pine ceiling sections were precut and pre-assembled. Instructions and all necessary hardware were included.

This gazebo is a 12-by-12-foot model, but 8-, 10-, and 14-foot units are also available. When buying a kit like this, you can also choose from a variety of roof designs, railings, corner braces, and other elements.

The unit shown was painted white after assembly. Because of the natural beauty of the clear redwood, a transparent stain or clear natural finish would also look great.

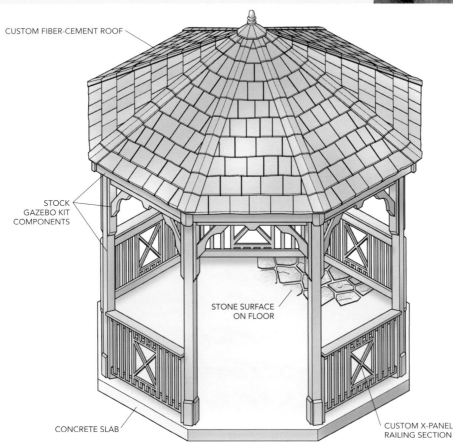

CUSTOM FIBER-CEMENT ROOF

STOCK GAZEBO KIT COMPONENTS

STONE SURFACE ON FLOOR

CONCRETE SLAB

CUSTOM X-PANEL RAILING SECTION

Project Spa Shelter

A great way to create a sense of privacy for an outdoor spa is to build an enclosure that includes an overhead. This elegantly simple spa structure does just that. It combines open-style roofing with a lattice screen to shelter the spa with style. Design: Ginette Gingras

Design Details

The structure's angular lines tie it to both the corner of the wooden deck and to the house's dramatic stone wall. Though this overhead was built for a spa in a wooden deck, the design could easily be adapted for a basic shelter on a patio.

The overhead's modest weight is borne by a ledger connected to the house's stone wall and three 4-by-4 posts that pass through the decking and stand on concrete footings and piers below the deck. For an alternate design, they could be fastened to post anchors on a patio slab. The corner posts are tied to the ledger and to a third post by 2-by-10 crossbeams. The 2-by-8 rafters have a decorative detail cut into their ends.

Building Notes

This unit was built at the same time as the deck construction and spa installation. That way, the builder could install the piers for the structure before the decking was in place.

To accomplish this project, you will need a helper and a pair of stepladders.

Be sure to treat all of the wood pieces with a preservative before installation, and treat any cut ends before placing the pieces. Although a stain can be applied to the entire unit after installation, it is usually easier to stain the pieces, assemble them, and then touch them up.

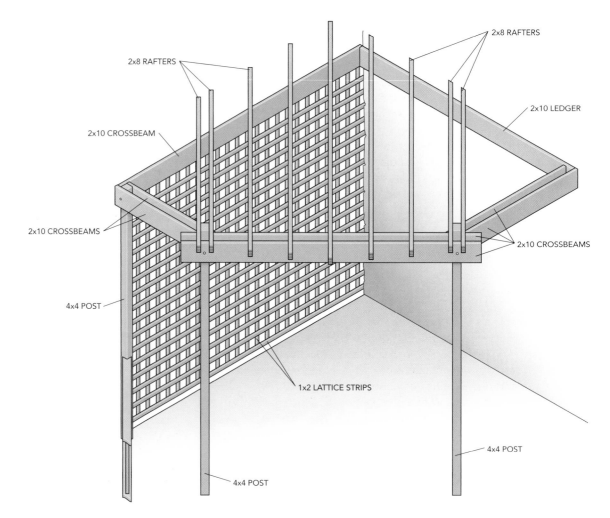

Step-By-Step

1 Begin by attaching the ledger to the house wall using 4-inch lag screws and masonry anchors, as discussed on page 59. Then, following the instructions on pages 55–56, lay out and pour the footings for the posts. Allow the concrete to cure.

2 Temporarily erect the 4-by-4 posts as discussed on page 69. With a single nail, tack each post to its post anchor, and then use a level to make sure the post is plumb. Temporarily brace each post with 1 by 3s.

3 Mark the top end of each post with a line that is level with the top of the ledger, as shown in the top photograph on page 70. Use a scrap from your 2-by-8 rafter stock to measure up from this line and make a second mark for cutting. Take down each post (noting where it goes), and complete the cutting line. Use a power circular saw to make the cut, as shown in the bottom photograph on page 70. After treating the cut end with preservative, return the post to its anchor, check it for plumb, brace it, and bolt it to the anchor.

4 Measure and cut the two 11-foot-long 2-by-10 crossbeams that run across the front of the unit. Raise the back-side crossbeam into place, align its top edge with those marks on the posts that are level with the ledger, and nail it to each post with two 16d galvanized nails placed 1 inch from the top and bottom edges of the board. Next, raise its mating crossbeam into position, and nail it the same way.

5 Next, add carriage bolts to secure the crossbeam-to-post connections. Using a power drill and an extra-long $\frac{1}{2}$-inch spade bit (or a standard bit with an extension shaft), center and drill a $\frac{1}{2}$-inch hole into the crossbeams and posts. With a hammer, tap in each 7-inch carriage bolt, add a washer, and tighten on a nut.

6 Measure and cut the crossbeam that runs above the lattice screen from the end of the ledger to the corner post (after making sure that the post is plumb). Drill pilot holes, and

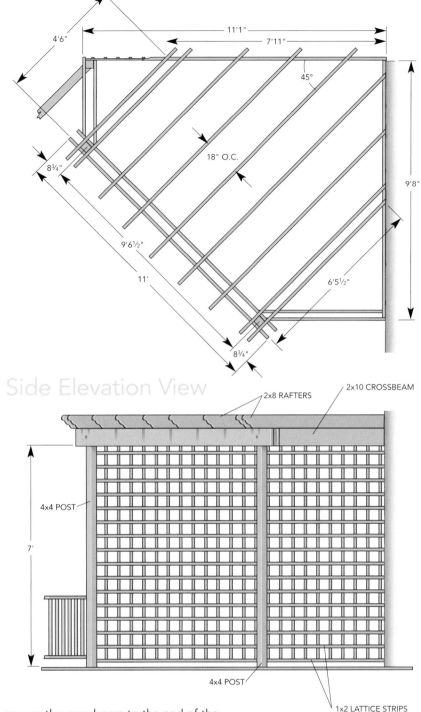

Plan View

Side Elevation View

2x8 RAFTERS

2x10 CROSSBEAM

4x4 POST

7'

4x4 POST

1x2 LATTICE STRIPS

11'1"

7'11"

45°

4'6"

8¾"

18" O.C.

9'6½"

11'

9'8"

6'5½"

8¾"

secure the crossbeam to the end of the ledger with two 4-inch lag screws.

7 Add the last four shorter crossbeams. Note that one end of each of these is cut at a 45-degree angle to fit snugly against the back side of the primary crossbeam. Fasten these pieces to the crossbeam and ledger with 10d galvanized nails and to the corner post with 16d galvanized nails and a one 7-inch carriage bolt.

Spa Shelter Materials Checklist

- Concrete & #4 rebar for footings
- 1x3 braces
- 4x4 posts
- 2x10 ledger & crossbeams
- 2x8 rafters
- 1x2 lattice strips
- Galvanized nails
- Carriage bolts, washers & nuts
- 4-inch lag screws & masonry anchors
- Deck screws
- Wood preservative & wood stain
- Sanding & finishing supplies

Front Elevation View

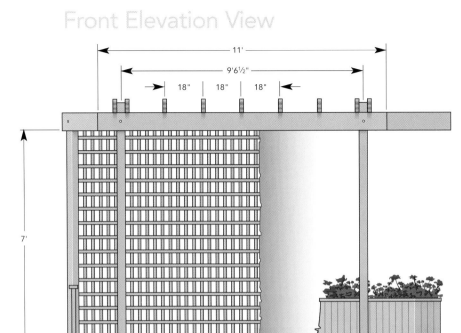

8 Measure, cut, and install the rafters. Note that the rafters have a decorative detail cut into the ends that overhang the front and side crossbeams. Where they butt up against the house wall, they are cut at a 45-degree angle. Measure and cut each of the rafters individually. You can vary the distance they overhang the crossbeam or maintain a consistent 5 inches. Utilize a compass to lay out a pleasing curve for the decorative detail, and then use a saber saw with a long blade to cut the form. After cutting one rafter, use it as a template for marking the other end cuts.

9 Treat the exposed ends with preservative, place the rafters on top of the crossbeams and ledger according to the plan view illustration on page 103, and then toenail them with 16d galvanized nails.

10 The lattice screen shown is custom-made from 1 by 2s placed on 6-inch centers. It is easiest to build the large panel flat on a level surface using a pneumatic nail gun with 1¼-inch nails for connecting the pieces. Alternatively, you can buy pre-made lattice panels, but, if you do this, you will need to install intermediate 2-by-4 posts to hide the seams between the panels.

Pool-Deck Pergola

This pergola stands nearly 9 feet above the 20-by-20-foot pool deck. A series of 4-by-4 posts supports an overhead framework made up of 2-by-10 beams, 2-by-6 rafters, and 1-by-2 lattice strips. However, the entire center of the pergola is wide open. This design detail—perimeter arbor with open center—lends an intimate, enclosed feeling to the backyard deck.

To create more shade for the lounging area around the pool, the 1-by-2 lattice strips could be placed closer together or replaced with wider 1 by 3s or 1 by 4s. Sunscreen fabric laid over the top of the lattice would provide full shade. The structure's members were finished first and then touched up after construction.

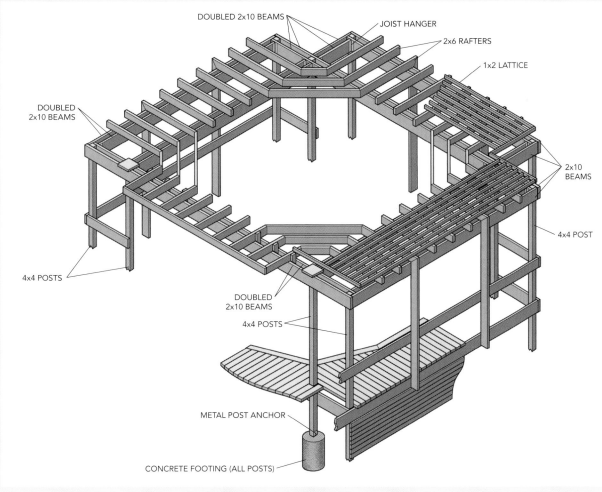

DOUBLED 2x10 BEAMS

JOIST HANGER

2x6 RAFTERS

1x2 LATTICE

DOUBLED 2x10 BEAMS

2x10 BEAMS

4x4 POSTS

4x4 POST

DOUBLED 2x10 BEAMS

4x4 POSTS

METAL POST ANCHOR

CONCRETE FOOTING (ALL POSTS)

Project | Tea Arbor

This charming arbor is guaranteed to draw you outdoors, whether for tea with a friend or some work on the laptop. The white-painted formal arbor is 80 inches wide, 38 inches deep, and 90 inches tall. It forms an inviting focal point, especially when it is tucked into a lushly planted area of the garden. Design: David Snow, English Arbor Company

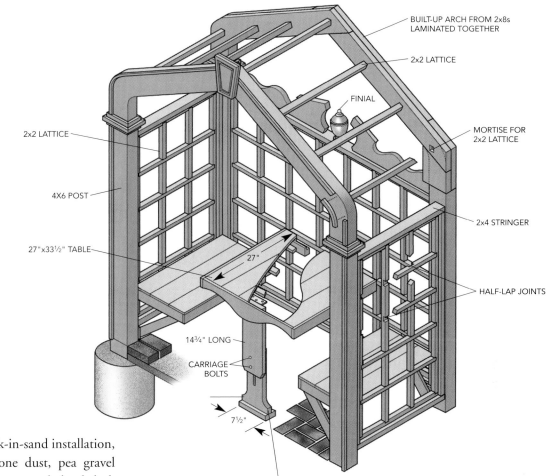

BUILT-UP ARCH FROM 2x8s LAMINATED TOGETHER

2x2 LATTICE

FINIAL

MORTISE FOR 2x2 LATTICE

2x2 LATTICE

4X6 POST

2x4 STRINGER

27"x33½" TABLE

27"

HALF-LAP JOINTS

14¾" LONG

CARRIAGE BOLTS

7½"

5"x17" ADJUSTABLE LEG

Design Details

The floor here is a brick-in-sand installation, but bluestone over stone dust, pea gravel over landscape fabric, or a grade-level deck using pressure-treated lumber would all be appropriate surfaces.

The elegant finial and pediments over the rear trellis, the trimmed arches, and the white paint finish are all classical elements that formalize the design. None require special woodworking skills or tools—just a portable jigsaw for cutting the arches and pediments. If you want to create your own profile, keep in mind the design relationship between the table apron's scrolled profile and the pediments. The finial can be purchased from a mail-order supply house for woodworkers.

The table is not only easily removable but the design also allows for adjustment of the leg to varying heights.

A painted arbor, especially one that supports vines, requires more maintenance than one that is oiled or stained. To get the most out of a paint job, apply wood preservative (especially on end grain), add primer prior to assembly, and finish with two topcoats of "lifetime" 100 percent acrylic latex paint.

Building Notes

For embedded posts, use pressure-treated lumber (but only for the posts) that is specified for "in-ground use." If you want to use redwood or cedar, install post anchors in the footings and shorten the posts to stand on top of the anchors to prevent direct contact with soil or concrete.

To laminate the arches, use waterproof glue, such as polyurethane, and sand well with 120-grit abrasive paper for an invisible (and less vulnerable) joint.

Long pipe clamps come in handy to draw the posts tight against the lattice frames as they are being fastened.

If your storage space is tight, consider attaching the upper portion of the table leg to the apron with carriage bolts and wing nuts so that you can disassemble it easily and store it efficiently.

Carefully fill all countersunk screw and nail holes after priming and before painting.

Plan View

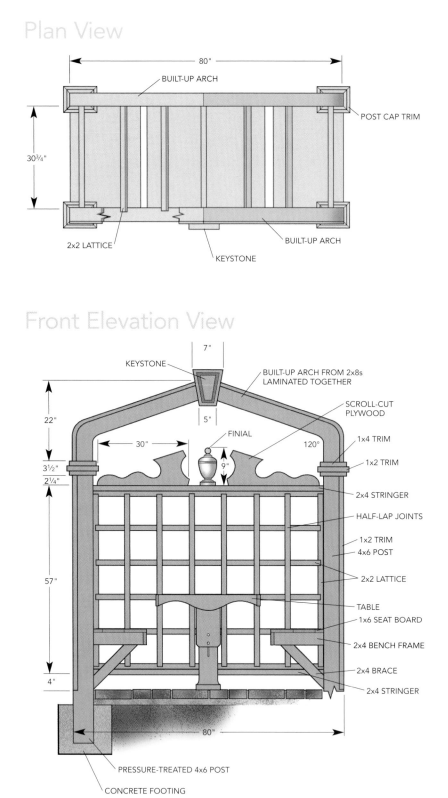

80"

BUILT-UP ARCH

POST CAP TRIM

30¾"

2x2 LATTICE

KEYSTONE

BUILT-UP ARCH

Front Elevation View

7"

KEYSTONE

BUILT-UP ARCH FROM 2x8s
LAMINATED TOGETHER

22"

5"

SCROLL-CUT
PLYWOOD

30"

FINIAL

120°

1x4 TRIM

3½"

1x2 TRIM

2¼"

9"

2x4 STRINGER

HALF-LAP JOINTS

1x2 TRIM

4x6 POST

57"

2x2 LATTICE

TABLE

1x6 SEAT BOARD

2x4 BENCH FRAME

4"

2x4 BRACE

2x4 STRINGER

80"

PRESSURE-TREATED 4x6 POST

CONCRETE FOOTING

Step-By-Step

1 Prepare the footings for embedded posts, making sure the footing tops fall below any planned patio or deck. Position the posts, and brace them with diagonal braces set between the tops of the posts and the stakes in the ground. When the concrete has cured, establish a level line across the tops of the posts and cut the posts to length.

2 Rip about ¹⁄₁₆ inch off the edges of 2-by-8 stock to square the edges. Cut the stock for each arch. Laminate each arch by applying waterproof glue to the two pieces, and then connect them with 2½-inch exterior screws.

3 Cut mortises on the inside face of each arch to receive the 2-by-2 roof lattice. Assemble the arches and lattice using construction adhesive and, with at least one helper, position the assembly atop the posts. Bore and countersink diagonal holes for screws through the arches and into the posts, and then fasten the arches.

4 Using a router and ³⁄₈-inch roundover bit, round the edges of the post-arch assemblies, except for the corners on the front face, which will be trimmed.

5 Mill and assemble the two side and rear lattice sections. Using a radial-arm saw and dado bit or a circular saw and chisel, cut half-lap joints in the 2-by-2 lattice stock. Toenail the assembly together using galvanized 4d finishing nails.

6 Cut the 2-by-4 stringers to length. Draw the profile of the pediments that go on top of the rear lattice onto two 2 by 10s, and make the scroll cuts with a jigsaw. Round over all but the bottom edges with a router, and then attach the pediments to the stringer from the underside with 3-inch screws.

7 Attach the stringers to the top and bottom of each lattice assembly using 2½-inch exterior screws on 6-inch centers. Install each assembly between the posts, and fasten them with screws that are driven diagonally through the stringers and into the posts.

8 Complete the trim work using galvanized finishing nails. First, trim the post-arch joint and cut, fabricate, and install the simulated keystone. Then trim the outer edge on the faces of the post-arch assemblies. Finally, bore a pilot hole for the finial lag screw and attach the finial.

9 Cut all the parts for both benches. Build the 2-by-4 frame, and attach the 1-by-6 seat and the diagonal braces. Position the assembled bench between the posts, level it, and secure the bench frame and braces to the posts with 2-inch screws.

10 Cut all the parts for the tabletop. Attach the cleat that supports the table's back edge to the rear trellis with 2½-inch screws. Secure the upper portion of the table leg to the front apron. Drill pilot holes, cut slots in the lower portion, and attach the 2-by-8 base. Join the two halves with a carriage bolt, washer, and nut. Position the table, and adjust the leg height to level.

Side Elevation View

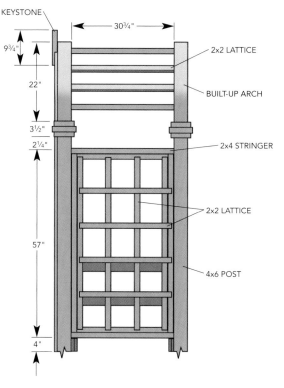

KEYSTONE

30¾"

9¾"

2x2 LATTICE

BUILT-UP ARCH

22"

3½"

2¼"

2x4 STRINGER

2x2 LATTICE

57"

4x6 POST

4"

Tea Arbor Materials Checklist

- Concrete & #4 rebar
- 4x6 posts, pressure-treated
- 2x6 for table leg
- 2x8s for arch & table leg
- 2x2 trellis stock
- 1x2 & 1x4 trim
- 2x10 pediments
- Decorative 1x8 keystone
- Decorative 9-inch finial
- 2x4 stringers, bench framing & braces
- 1x3 table aprons
- 1x6 for table top, bench seat & apron
- Waterproof glue
- Galvanized nails & outdoor screws
- Galvanized carriage bolts, washers & nuts
- Sanding & finishing supplies
- Paint, stain, or wood preservative

Cedar Cathedral

Agrove of lanky cedar trees provides an apt setting for this garden gazebo. Groups of cedar posts support built-in benches and the open rafter roof. Between the posts at the ends of the benches are built-in planters. A series of 1 by 2s wrap the post tops, creating texture as well as visual interest. The 2-by-6 rafters overlap at the ridge, and 1 by 4s nailed to each side of the rafters add detail.

Trim is fitted to the bottom of the posts at deck level; the posts, however, continue down beneath the gazebo's decking, where they are supported by footings as required by code.

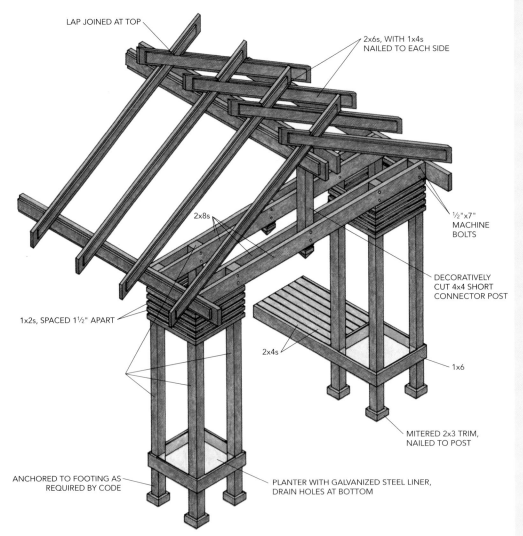

LAP JOINED AT TOP

2x6s, WITH 1x4s NAILED TO EACH SIDE

2x8s

½"x7" MACHINE BOLTS

DECORATIVELY CUT 4x4 SHORT CONNECTOR POST

1x2s, SPACED 1½" APART

2x4s

1x6

MITERED 2x3 TRIM, NAILED TO POST

ANCHORED TO FOOTING AS REQUIRED BY CODE

PLANTER WITH GALVANIZED STEEL LINER, DRAIN HOLES AT BOTTOM

Project Traditional Trellis

Measuring 47 feet long, this trellis shades the patio, directly accessible from the dining room, living room, and kitchen. The substantial trellis was carefully designed to be in scale and style with the architectural details of the house.
Architect: Jared Polsky & Associates

Symmetry and classical lines tie this massive trellis into the home's traditional architecture.

Design Details

Though massive, the dimensions of this trellis—15-inch-diameter columns, 8-by-10 beams, 4-by-7 purlins, and 3-by-3 topmost cross members—can easily be scaled down to be suitable for the size and trim details of a smaller home.

Vines planted at the base of the two double columns reach out across the top of the trellis and up a second-floor-balcony railing. They provide dense shade in summer, but when their foliage drops in winter, they allow warming sunlight to pass into the house. The columns stand on a bluestone-capped patio.

Though the homeowners chose a painted finish, if you intend to grow vines on your trellis, a stained finish may be more practical.

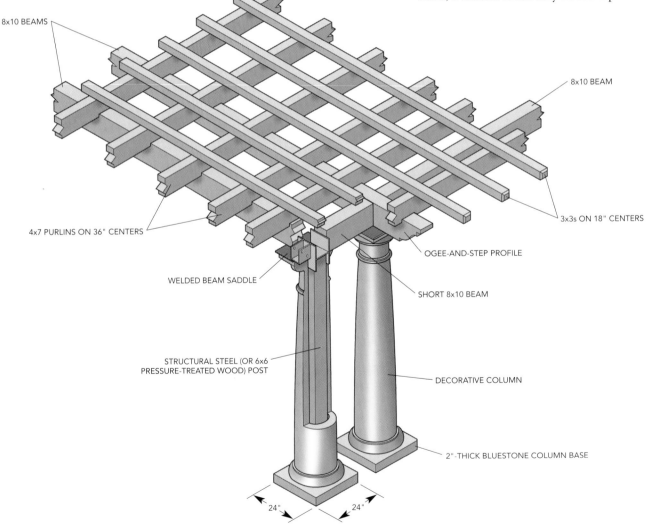

8x10 BEAMS

8x10 BEAM

4x7 PURLINS ON 36" CENTERS

3x3s ON 18" CENTERS

OGEE-AND-STEP PROFILE

WELDED BEAM SADDLE

SHORT 8x10 BEAM

STRUCTURAL STEEL (OR 6x6 PRESSURE-TREATED WOOD) POST

DECORATIVE COLUMN

2"-THICK BLUESTONE COLUMN BASE

24"   24"

Building Notes

Decorative columns are available as whole columns that fit over structural posts, or they can be split at the mill or on site and then wrapped around structural posts. A significant advantage of split columns is that they are relatively easy to install.

Steel posts were used for this trellis, but the overall design could be modified to employ more-conventional 6-by-6 pressure-treated wood posts.

The beams were secured to metal anchors mounted with bolts through flashed ledger blocks into the house's framing. To create a perfectly waterproof connection, a nailable waterproof membrane was used to extend copper flashing on all sides.

The short, nonstructural beams extending from the house at the ends were simply scribed and cut to fit into the roof fascia. If your beams similarly need to be scribed, make a plywood template and verify a good joint before tracing the shape onto and cutting the beams. Be sure to prime all wood before it is assembled.

Step-By-Step

1 Form the column footings up to grade level, and embed the custom-welded post bases in the concrete so that their tops are 1¾ inches above the ground. When the concrete is cured, position and plumb each post before welding it to its base.

2 Spread mortar at the base of each post, lay in 2-inch-square bluestone rods, and fill in the area with concrete. Lay a mortar setting bed, and then lower the 2-inch-thick, 2-foot-square beveled bluestone column bases down over the posts.

3 Weld the saddles on the tops of the posts. Temporarily position 2 by 4s in the saddles and against the house to ensure that the saddles are perpendicular to the house wall. If whole columns are utilized, the bases, columns, and caps must be placed over the posts before the welding. Install blocking between the column interior and the posts according to the instructions provided by the manufacturer.

4 Screw the ledger blocks onto the sheathing wall, and cover the sheathing with a bituminous membrane. Install copper flashing up the wall and over the top of the ledger, and then lap building paper over the flashing. Bolt steel anchors through the blocks into the framing.

5 Cut and sand all the lumber. Brush on or soak the members in wood preservative, and then apply primer. As construction progresses, carefully plug or fill all fastener holes. When construction is complete, apply "lifetime" 100 percent exterior acrylic-latex paint.

6 Using a plywood template, cut and mill the ogee-and-step profile on the outer ends of the beams that extend from the house. Mortise channels in the underside of the beams at the column end and at the house end to accept the steel anchors. Position the beams, and then locate the clearance holes for the bolts. Counterbore and bore the holes, and then install the bolts, nuts, and washers.

7 Attach the short beams between the paired columns to the carrying beams with screws installed diagonally into bored and countersunk holes. Mortise channels in the underside of the remaining beams at both ends to fit over the steel anchors and bolts, as before.

Traditional Trellis Materials Checklist

- Concrete, #4 rebar & form lumber
- Columns, bases & caps
- 2-inch-by-2-foot-square beveled bluestone column bases
- Ledger blocks
- Steel posts or 6x6 pressure-treated posts
- 8x10 beams
- 4x7 purlins
- 3x3 trellis stock
- Bituminous membrane
- Building paper
- Copper flashing
- Caulking compound
- Galvanized nails & outdoor screws
- Galvanized lag screws & washers
- Galvanized machine bolts, washers & nuts
- Custom steel post anchors & beam saddles
- Sanding & finishing supplies
- Wood preservative
- Exterior primer
- Acrylic-latex exterior paint

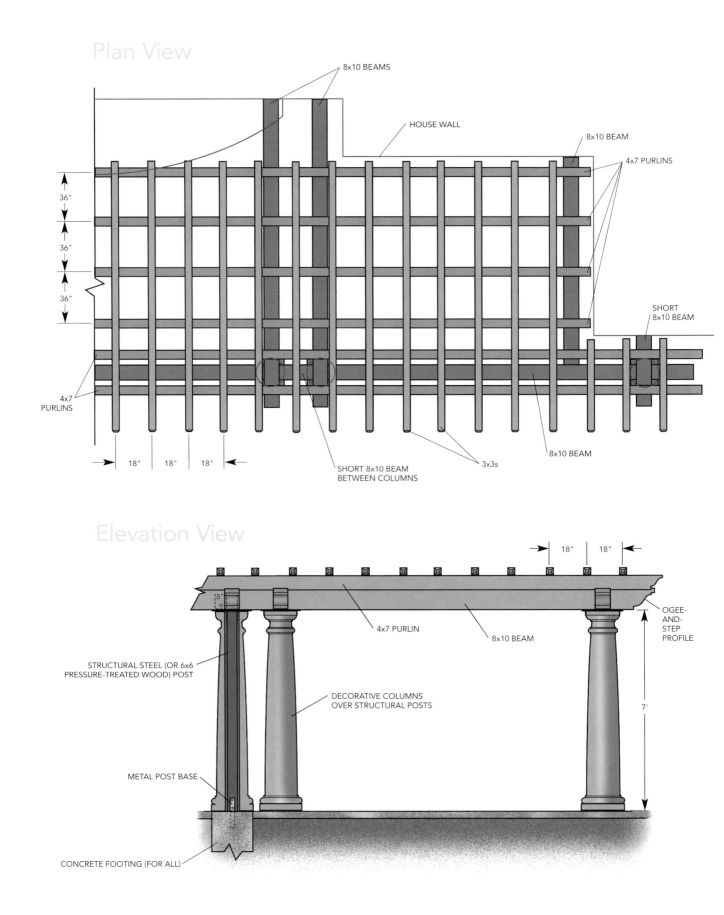

Plan View

8x10 BEAMS

HOUSE WALL

8x10 BEAM

4x7 PURLINS

36"

36"

36"

SHORT
8x10 BEAM

4x7
PURLINS

18" 18" 18"

SHORT 8x10 BEAM
BETWEEN COLUMNS

3x3s

8x10 BEAM

Elevation View

18" 18"

4x7 PURLIN

8x10 BEAM

OGEE-
AND-
STEP
PROFILE

STRUCTURAL STEEL (OR 6x6
PRESSURE-TREATED WOOD) POST

DECORATIVE COLUMNS
OVER STRUCTURAL POSTS

7'

METAL POST BASE

CONCRETE FOOTING (FOR ALL)

8 Lay purlins 36 inches on center across the beams so end joints are centered over a beam. Mark the underside of the purlins at the point at which they intersect the beams, and then cut 1-inch-deep notches in the purlins to fit over the beams. Bore and countersink for screws angled through the purlins into the tops of the beams.

9 Mill the 3-by-3 topmost cross members, and chamfer their ends. Install them across the tops of the purlins on 18-inch centers with outdoor screws.

10 If split columns, bases, and caps are planned, install them around the posts according to the instructions provided by the manufacturer. Use waterproof glue and stainless-steel fasteners, making sure there is no direct contact between non-pressure-treated wood and concrete or stone. Flash the tops of the wood caps, leaving the center open for ventilation.

Shaded Entry

Lattice panels run the length of the house, forming a shaded gallery for walking and sitting. Because the house itself provides structural stability for the overhead, construction is simple, despite the project's large scale.

The 4-by-4 posts, anchored to concrete footings, are made from decay-resistant redwood. Outside posts have 2 by 3s nailed to each face; interior posts have 1-by-12 trim, mitered at the corners, nailed to their bases.

Heavy-duty framing anchors connect beams where they intersect. The prefabricated lattice panels, cut to fit, are placed on 2 by 2s nailed along the beams.

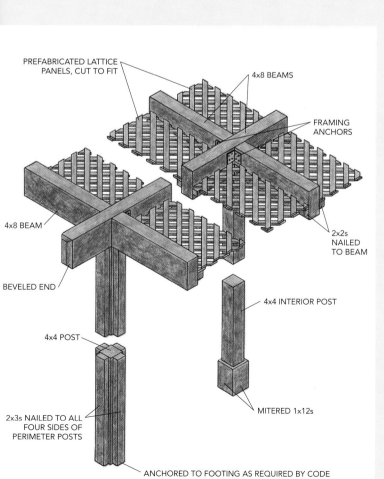

PREFABRICATED LATTICE PANELS, CUT TO FIT

4x8 BEAMS

FRAMING ANCHORS

4x8 BEAM

2x2s NAILED TO BEAM

BEVELED END

4x4 INTERIOR POST

4x4 POST

MITERED 1x12s

2x3s NAILED TO ALL FOUR SIDES OF PERIMETER POSTS

ANCHORED TO FOOTING AS REQUIRED BY CODE

Project Open Shelter

Conveniently located just a few steps from the house, this 10-by-14½-foot arbor invites family and friends outdoors to dine or otherwise enjoy the deck and garden space. The structure is located in the middle of three cascading decks that make the transition from the floor level of the house to the driveway and garden. Landscape architect: J. Starbuck

Design Details

The use of three 6-by-6 posts at each corner defines the room-like space, making railings unnecessary. If your structure is elevated or on a hillside, a railing made with a 2-by-6 top rail, 2-by-2 spindles on 4½-inch centers, and a 2-by-4 bottom rail can easily be attached on one or more sides. The area underneath can be framed with lattice for additional enclosure, to hide unwanted views, or simply to serve as a decorative element.

If, as in this case, your arbor serves as a dining area, make sure the dimensions of your dining table and chairs permit easy passage around them. This design offers expanded walking room because the deck extends several feet past the arbor and has wide, low-rise stairs.

Trim details at the post tops and on the roof fascia add a distinctive touch.

Building Notes

This arbor can be built over a grade-level or elevated deck or over a patio. If the deck is being constructed at the same time, it may be able to share common footings and posts with the arbor.

Capping the posts with 2 by 6s not only secures the posts together but also protects their end grain from absorbing moisture.

Because the roof framing is exposed to the elements, tight joints are particularly important for appearance' sake. This handsome design calls for a backed-up hip rafter or ridge board ripped to width so that one edge is flush with the bottom of the rafters and the other edge is beveled to align with the top of the rafters. Even though wind uplift is not a factor for this open arbor, using bolts, long screws, and/or long nails instead of less attractive framing hardware is well worth the increased labor involved.

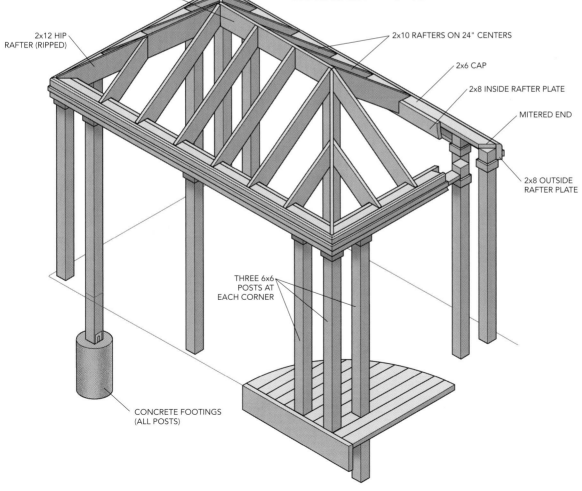

2x12 RIDGE RAFTER

2x12 HIP RAFTER (RIPPED)

2x10 RAFTERS ON 24" CENTERS

2x6 CAP

2x8 INSIDE RAFTER PLATE

MITERED END

2x8 OUTSIDE RAFTER PLATE

THREE 6x6 POSTS AT EACH CORNER

CONCRETE FOOTINGS (ALL POSTS)

Plan View

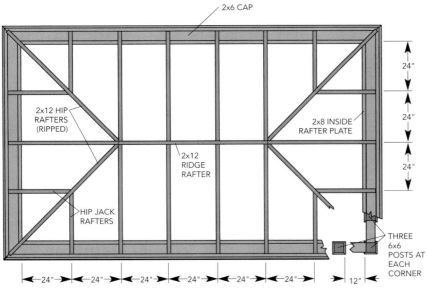

2x6 CAP

2x12 HIP RAFTERS (RIPPED)

2x8 INSIDE RAFTER PLATE

2x12 RIDGE RAFTER

HIP JACK RAFTERS

THREE 6x6 POSTS AT EACH CORNER

24" 24" 24" 24" 24" 24" 24" 24" 24"

12"

Elevation View

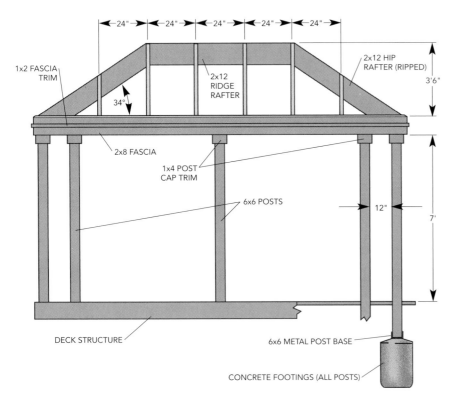

24" 24" 24" 24" 24"

1x2 FASCIA TRIM

2x12 HIP RAFTER (RIPPED)

3'6"

2x12 RIDGE RAFTER

34°

2x8 FASCIA

1x4 POST CAP TRIM

6x6 POSTS

12"

7'

DECK STRUCTURE

6x6 METAL POST BASE

CONCRETE FOOTINGS (ALL POSTS)

Step-By-Step

1 Form and pour the footings. Embed post anchors in each footing to accept the columns. To prevent moisture absorption through the end grain, make sure the posts do not sit directly on the concrete.

2 Cut the 6-by-6 posts to length, and secure them to the post bases with bolts. Nail 2-by-6 caps, mitered at the outside corners, across the post tops. Brace all posts diagonally in both directions to hold them plumb.

3 Next, for the two narrow "sides" of the structure, cut 2-by-8 inside rafter plates to lengths equal to the outside dimension of the posts' spans. Clamp them to the inner faces of the post tops, making them flush with the 2-by-6 post caps, while you drill countersink and clearance holes. Fasten the inside rafter plates to the posts with bolts, washers, and nuts (or lag bolts).

4 For the long "sides," cut the inside rafter plates to fit between the already installed rafter plates and join them by end nailing. Clamp the rafter plates to the posts that are at mid-span, double-check that the posts are plumb, and then drill for and install bolts as before.

5 Cut the angles on the top and bottom of the six common rafters so that they fit flush with the outsides of the posts and against the 2-by-12 ridge rafter. Cut the bird's-mouth notches so that each rafter fits over the 2-by-8 inside rafter plate.

6 Brace the ridge board in place while you attach the rafters to it and to the 2-by-8 fascia. Next, cut, notch, and install the two common rafters at the center of each hip roof, and attach them to the end of the ridge board and the rafter plate.

7 Using a framing square, determine the length and cutting angles for the 2-by-12 hip rafters. Cut and install the four hip rafters, which require double side cuts at both top and bottom. Make the cuts that form the bird's-mouth.

8 Next, cut, notch, and install the hip jack rafters. The top angle must have a single side cut where it meets the hip rafter. The length of these rafters must be shortened by half the 45-degree thickness of the hip rafter (about 1$\frac{1}{16}$ inches).

9 Rip the bevel along the top edge of the 2-by-8 fascia boards. Cut them to length, miter the corners, and nail them to the ends of all the rafters and corner posts. Install the 1-by-2 fascia trim and 1-by-4 post cap trim with exterior adhesive and 8d galvanized nails (miter at corners).

10 Perform any final sanding that may be needed, and apply a suitable exterior stain.

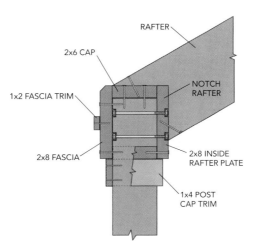

RAFTER

2x6 CAP

1x2 FASCIA TRIM

NOTCH RAFTER

2x8 FASCIA

2x8 INSIDE RAFTER PLATE

1x4 POST CAP TRIM

Open Shelter Materials Checklist

- Concrete, #4 rebar & form lumber for footings
- 6x6 posts
- 2x6 post caps
- 2x8 rafter plates & fascia
- 2x10 & 2x12 rafters
- 1x2 & 1x4 trim
- Exterior adhesive
- Galvanized nails & outdoor screws
- Galvanized machine bolts, washers & nuts
- Metal post anchors
- Metal framing brackets & fasteners
- Sanding & finishing supplies
- Paint, stain, or wood preservative

Rustic Retreat

Another take on the open shelter concept, this simple square structure serves as a shady place for reading and relaxation, quiet contemplation or conversation.

Standing on an exposed aggregate slab, the structure was built from sturdy "construction heart" redwood. It was brushed with bleaching oil for an immediate driftwood-gray effect.

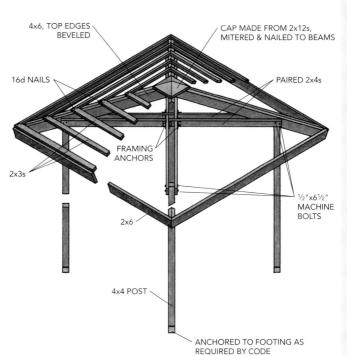

4x6, TOP EDGES BEVELED

CAP MADE FROM 2x12s, MITERED & NAILED TO BEAMS

16d NAILS

PAIRED 2x4s

FRAMING ANCHORS

2x3s

2x6

$\frac{1}{2}$" x 6$\frac{1}{2}$" MACHINE BOLTS

4x4 POST

ANCHORED TO FOOTING AS REQUIRED BY CODE

Designer's Sketchbook

Project | Simple Square Structure

This owner-built 8-foot-square trellis, floored with flagstone and furnished with comfortable chairs, provides an inviting place to relax and enjoy the view from a hillside garden. Without a doubt, this handsome structure also enhances the view of the garden from the house.

Landscape architect: Lankford Associates

Design Details

Pressure-treated posts, though ideal for durability (especially below grade), inevitably check, or crack. While checking does not affect strength, it is particularly unsightly when the wood is painted. Capping the posts with boards more suitable for painting, such as better grades of pine or redwood, gives this structure the benefits of both types of wood. In addition, the fascia provides a ledge for the 2-by-8 beams, effectively eliminating the need for bolted connections.

The architectural details at the ends of the front and rear beams can be adapted to blend with design elements of your home or garden. Before cutting the beams, experiment with shaped plywood patterns tacked onto the ends of uncut 2-bys.

Building Notes

Cut the posts in place after erecting them. Lay out the positions of the crossing 2-by-4 trellis pieces, and then mark the tops of the lower ones for the overlapping pieces. Cut the fascia boards so they will end a couple of inches above a concrete patio and even more above soil or plants. After cutting the posts' 1-by-8 fascia boards, soak the ends in a wood preservative to protect the end grain from moisture damage.

To install the two side beams, tack cleats onto posts 7¼ inches down from the top.

Cut the notches in the trellis 2 by 4s with a jigsaw, using the first board as a template for the others; or, clamp the 2 by 4s side by side for gang cutting with a circular saw.

Prime all the cut lumber before installing it. Use a drum sander or sanding attachment to smooth the end grain of the ogee cuts on the long beams. Countersink all nails, and then fill the holes with exterior filler prior to applying the finish coat.

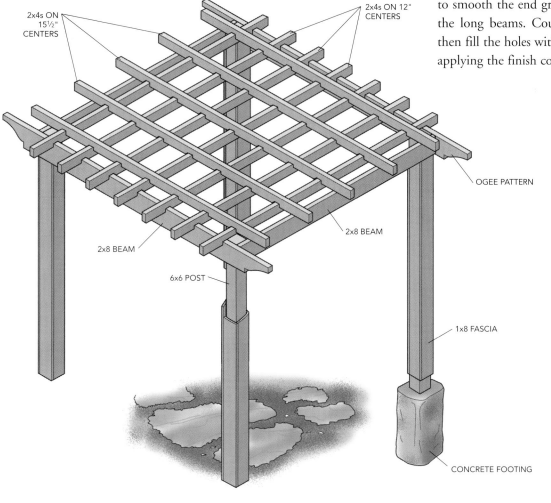

2x4s ON 15½" CENTERS

2x4s ON 12" CENTERS

OGEE PATTERN

2x8 BEAM

2x8 BEAM

6x6 POST

1x8 FASCIA

CONCRETE FOOTING

Plan View

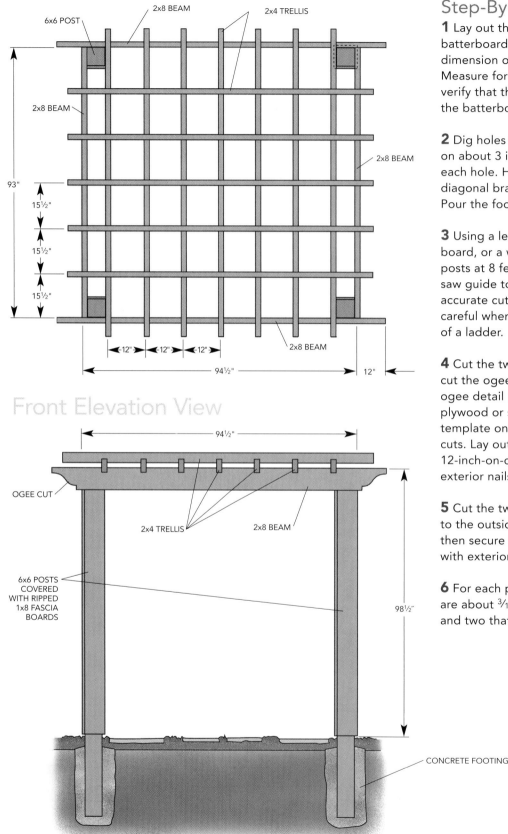

6x6 POST

2x8 BEAM

2x4 TRELLIS

2x8 BEAM

2x8 BEAM

93"

15½"

15½"

15½"

12" 12" 12"

2x8 BEAM

94½"

12"

Front Elevation View

94½"

OGEE CUT

2x4 TRELLIS

2x8 BEAM

6x6 POSTS COVERED WITH RIPPED 1x8 FASCIA BOARDS

98½"

CONCRETE FOOTING

Step-By-Step

1 Lay out the post locations by using batterboards and string so that the outside dimension of each "side" is 94½ inches. Measure for equal diagonal dimensions to verify that the structure will be square. Mark the batterboards.

2 Dig holes for the footings. Set each post on about 3 inches of gravel at the bottom of each hole. Hold the posts plumb by placing diagonal braces at right angles to each other. Pour the footings.

3 Using a level and an 8-foot-long straight board, or a water level, mark the tops of the posts at 8 feet, 2½ inches. Clamp or tack a saw guide to the posts to ensure a safe and accurate cut with a circular saw. Be very careful when cutting while standing on top of a ladder.

4 Cut the two long beams to length, and cut the ogee detail. Make a template for the ogee detail by using a jigsaw and ¼-inch plywood or similar scrap. Then clamp the template onto the beams to guide your cuts. Lay out the tops of the beams for the 12-inch-on-center 2 by 4s. Secure them with exterior nails or screws.

5 Cut the two side beams to length—equal to the outside post-to-post distance—and then secure the beams flush to the post tops with exterior nails or screws.

6 For each post, rip two fascia boards that are about ³⁄₁₆ inch wider than the post width and two that are 1½ inches wider than these.

7 Cut a ¾-by-7¼-inch notch at the top of one inside-corner fascia board for each post so it will fit around the beam. Nail the two outside-corner boards together, and then secure them to the posts; do the same for the inside-corner boards.

8 Cut the lower 2-by-4 trellis members to length. Lay one across the top of the long beams on one end, center it for an equal overhang on each side, and then mark the 1-by-1½-inch notches where the member crosses the two beams. Use this piece as a template for cutting the notches in the other 2 by 4s that run this direction.

9 Cut the top 2-by-4 trellis members to length. Locate and cut the notches in the bottoms of them as you did for those in the first course. Predrill pilot holes, and then toenail the members onto the tops of the first course of trellis.

10 Sand the fascia, and ease the corners to eliminate any splinters. Touch up the primer as needed, and apply a topcoat of 100 percent acrylic latex paint to the entire structure.

Simple Square Structure Materials Checklist

- Concrete, #4 rebar & form lumber for footings
- Gravel
- 6x6 posts, pressure-treated
- 2x8 beams
- 2x4 trellis stock
- 1x8 trim
- Galvanized nails & outdoor screws
- Sanding & finishing supplies
- Paint, stain, or wood preservative

Solid Shelter

Stuccoed columns supporting an overhead declare durability and strength and define the space with authority. The stuccoed columns shown here support two 4-by-10 beams, decoratively cut at the ends. The beams hold a series of five 3-by-8 beams on 36-inch centers.

The open-style roofing is made from 3 by 4s, spaced 9 inches on center and mounted with lag screws and heavy-duty galvanized metal anchors that are set an inch down from the top of the 3-by-8 beams.

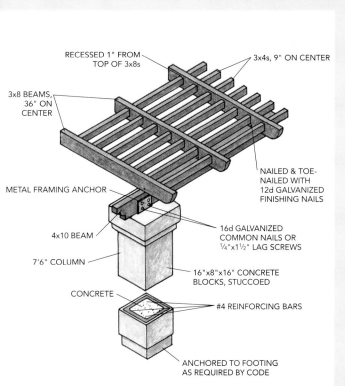

RECESSED 1" FROM TOP OF 3x8s

3x4s, 9" ON CENTER

3x8 BEAMS, 36" ON CENTER

NAILED & TOE-NAILED WITH 12d GALVANIZED FINISHING NAILS

METAL FRAMING ANCHOR

4x10 BEAM

7'6" COLUMN

16d GALVANIZED COMMON NAILS OR ¼"x1½" LAG SCREWS

16"x8"x16" CONCRETE BLOCKS, STUCCOED

CONCRETE

#4 REINFORCING BARS

ANCHORED TO FOOTING AS REQUIRED BY CODE

Designer's Sketchbook

Project House-Attached Overhead

Casting partial shade on a generously sized poolside deck, this classic overhead is the perfect complement to the house's traditional style. Though the overhead is fairly simple in structure, it gains its charm from four robust architectural columns and a system of intricately detailed rafters that repeat along its length. Design: Dan Haslegrave

Design Details

The overhead is supported by a ledger connected to the house wall and by four 6-by-6 posts that are concealed inside decorative 8-foot fiberglass columns. The posts stand on typical concrete piers and footings below the deck (see page 61). If you are building on a patio instead of a deck, you may be able to anchor the posts directly on the slab. For more about this, see pages 60–61.

Be sure to follow the column manufacturer's instructions and specifications for proper assembly and anchoring.

Building Notes

For cutting the decorative rafter tails, you will need a saber saw and several sharp, long wood-cutting blades. You will also need a ⅜-inch power drill for drilling pilot holes into the beams. And plan to have on hand a pair of stepladders and a helper.

Because of the repeating theme of this design, construction is straightforward. Plan to cut all of the rafters at one time. When you do this, lay out and cut the first one, and then use it as a pattern for marking and cutting the remaining ones. Always be sure to double-check the foundation layout before cutting any material.

Note that columns like these usually come white and split into halves that are then glued together with special adhesive once installed. Be sure to study the manufacturer's instructions before beginning construction, and, if need be, make modifications to the following directions accordingly.

Prime and paint all of the components—including the joist hangers for connecting the rafters to the ledger—before assembly to save yourself considerable labor later on. Then just touch up the paint after the structure is built.

House-Attached Overhead Materials Checklist

- Concrete & #4 rebar for footings
- 8-foot fiberglass columns
- 6x6 pressure-treated posts
- Joist hangers
- 2x10 crossbeams, rafters & ledger
- 1x3 lattice strips
- Galvanized nails
- Lag screws & washers
- Wood primer & paint
- Sanding & finishing supplies

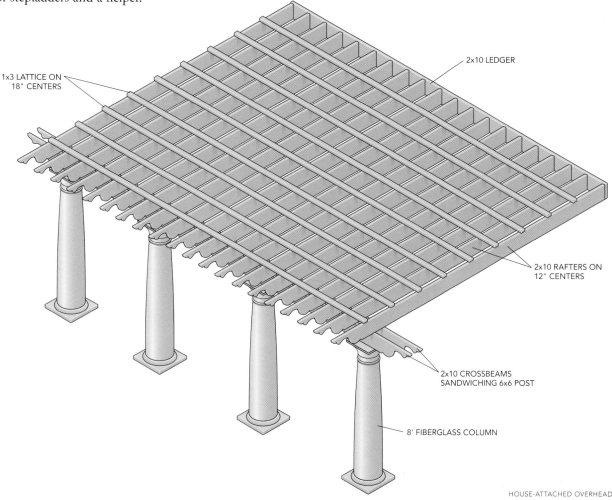

1x3 LATTICE ON 18" CENTERS

2x10 LEDGER

2x10 RAFTERS ON 12" CENTERS

2x10 CROSSBEAMS SANDWICHING 6x6 POST

8' FIBERGLASS COLUMN

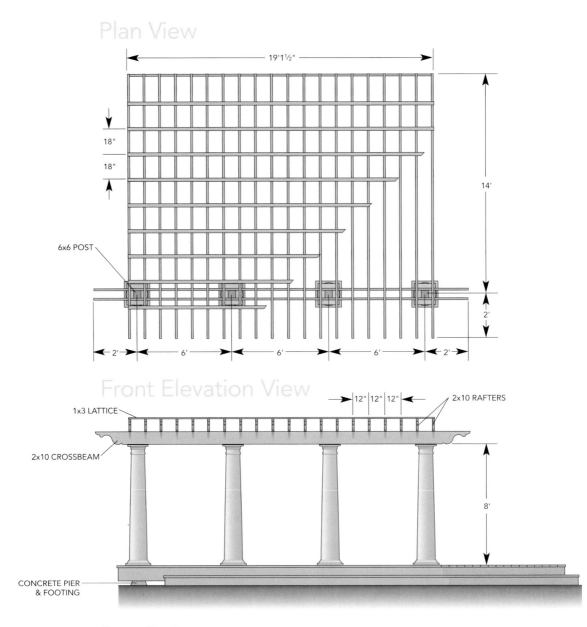

Plan View

19'1½"

18"

18"

14'

6x6 POST

2'

2' — 6' — 6' — 6' — 2'

Front Elevation View

1x3 LATTICE

2x10 CROSSBEAM

12" 12" 12"

2x10 RAFTERS

8'

CONCRETE PIER
& FOOTING

Step-By-Step

1 Begin by attaching the ledger to the house wall's framing as discussed on page 58. Then, following the directions given on pages 65–66, pour the concrete footings using 6-by-6 post anchors.

2 Temporarily install the 6-by-6 posts in their anchors as discussed on page 69. Use a level to make sure each one is plumb. Support each post in its position with the help of 1-by-3 temporary diagonal braces.

3 Mark the top end of each post with a cutting line that is level with the bottom of the ledger, using the methods discussed on page 70. Take the posts down one at a time, and then use a power circular saw and a handsaw to cut them off (also shown

on page 70). Treat all of the cut ends with preservative, allow them to dry, and then return each post to its anchor. Check the first one for plumb, brace it, and then fasten it to its anchor with 1½-inch lag screws. Repeat for the posts.

4 Assemble the fiberglass columns around the posts according to the manufacturer's instructions. Cap the columns and post tops with sheet-metal flashing.

5 Measure and cut to length the two 22-foot-long 2-by-10 crossbeams that connect the columns. Mark a pattern for the decorative detail at the end of one crossbeam, using a compass and a square. Cut this end, and then use it as a pattern for marking the other ends.

6 Along with a helper, raise the back-side crossbeam into place, aligning its top edge with the top of the posts. Check it for level, make any necessary adjustments, and then nail it to each post with two 16d galvanized nails placed ¾ inch from the crossbeam's top and bottom edges. Lift the mating crossbeam into position, and nail it the same way.

7 Secure the crossbeams to the posts with ⅜-by-4-inch lag screws and washers after first drilling pilot holes. Next, center the lag screws on the posts, and space them about 1½ inches from the crossbeams' top and bottom edges. Thread a washer onto each lag screw before driving it in.

8 Mark the placement of the rafters on the ledger and the top of the crossbeams according to the plan-view illustration. Then, mount the joist hangers on the ledger with approved galvanized nails.

9 Cut the rafters and the decorative profile of their ends, and prime and paint the cut ends. Then lift the rafters up into the brackets, align them with their marks on the crossbeams, and secure them to the hangers with approved galvanized nails. Toenail each rafter to each crossbeam with a 16d galvanized nail on each side.

10 Mark the tops of the end rafters for placement of the 1-by-3 lattice strips. Position the 1 by 3s, making sure they overhang equally at both ends, and nail them to the tops of the rafters with two 8d galvanized nails per rafter. Prime and touch up the structure with paint, as needed.

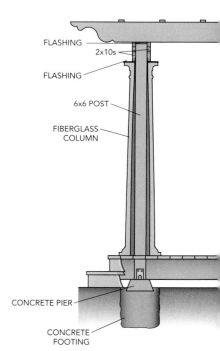

FLASHING
2x10s
FLASHING
6x6 POST
FIBERGLASS COLUMN
CONCRETE PIER
CONCRETE FOOTING

Bold Sun Shelter

This sound overhead provides both a feeling of enclosure and an escape from the heat and glare of the strong afternoon sun.

Doubled 3-by-8 beams running parallel to the house are bolted to the sides of the posts. From a 2-by-8 ledger lag-screwed to the house wall, doubled 4-by-8 beams hang from short connector posts. Shade is thrown by 2-by-4s on edge, spaced 6 inches center to center. Because the overhead is attached to the house, cross bracing is not necessary.

Posts are built out with 2 by 4s on each face. To soften the lines, beam and post edges are beveled.

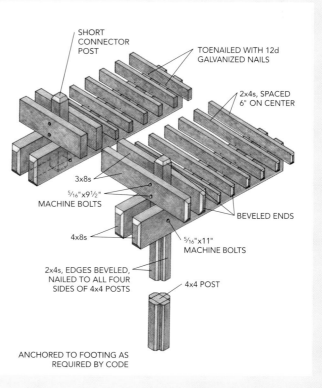

SHORT CONNECTOR POST
TOENAILED WITH 12d GALVANIZED NAILS
2x4s, SPACED 6" ON CENTER
3x8s
5/16"x9½" MACHINE BOLTS
BEVELED ENDS
4x8s
5/16"x11" MACHINE BOLTS
2x4s, EDGES BEVELED, NAILED TO ALL FOUR SIDES OF 4x4 POSTS
4x4 POST
ANCHORED TO FOOTING AS REQUIRED BY CODE

Designer's Sketchbook

Project | Corner Gazebo Bench

Elegantly framing the corner of a redwood deck, this charming L-shaped gazebo offers comfortable seating for conversation o[r] quiet contemplation. The white-painted structure has a distinct[ive] hip roof made up of mitered 2 by 2s. Designer: Mark Hajjar

Design Details

Built entirely of redwood, this cozy corner gazebo measures approximately 10 feet by 10 feet. The oversized benches are a generous 36 inches deep (nearly twice as deep as most outdoor benches) so there's ample room for lounging. Foam seat cushions covered with all-weather fabric add comfort and style. Diagonal-pattern lattice is used across the backs of the benches to create an open, airy feeling. If your lumber dealer does not carry redwood in all of the sizes used for this gazebo, you can substitute with other species as long as you paint the structure.

The gazebo's frame consists of five 4-by-4 posts, which support 4-by-6 beams. The beams, in turn, support 2-by-4 roof rafters spaced 24 inches on center. The 2-by-2 slats nailed across the rafters are spaced 4 inches on center. This "open roof" design allows some sun to shine through yet provides enough shade to keep the gazebo cool.

Building Notes

According to code, adding this gazebo to an existing deck requires passing the five posts through the decking and setting them on concrete footings. If the gazebo is part of a new deck plan, reinforce the understructure with additional posts and double joists, and then fasten the gazebo posts directly to the deck's framing with carriage bolts. (If your gazebo will sit on a concrete patio, secure it using post anchors and masonry fasteners.)

To create strong, solid joints, join the timbers of the 4-by-6 frame that supports the roof rafters with metal framing anchors.

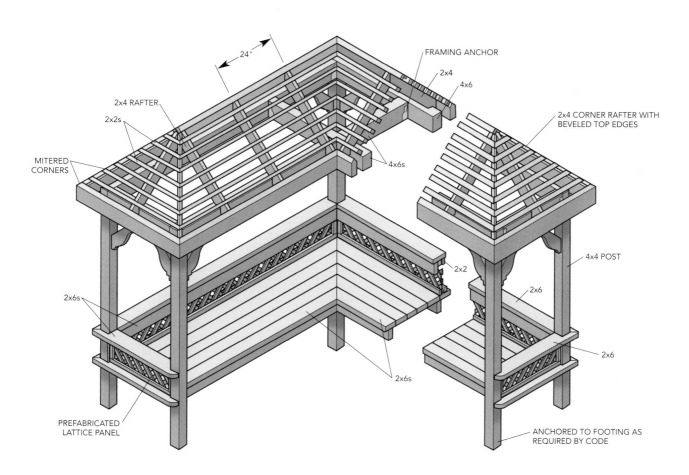

Partial Section Elevation

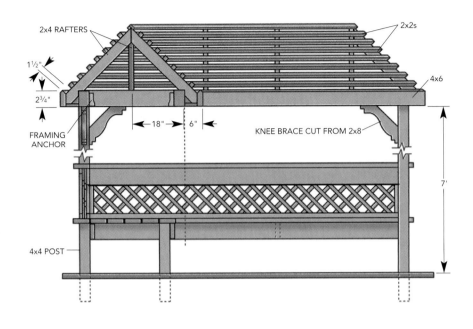

2x4 RAFTERS

2x2s

1½"

2¾"

FRAMING ANCHOR

18"   6"

KNEE BRACE CUT FROM 2x8

4x6

7'

4x4 POST

Plan View

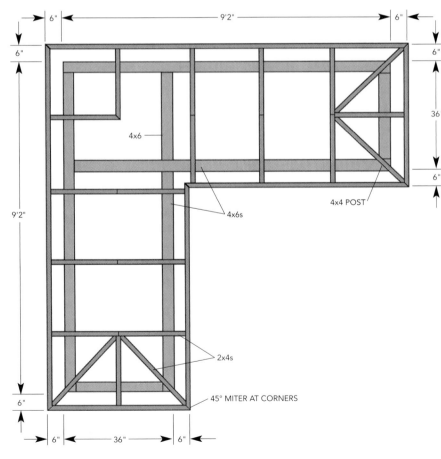

6"

9'2"

6"

6"

6"

4x6

36"

6"

4x6s

4x4 POST

9'2"

2x4s

45° MITER AT CORNERS

6"

6"   36"   6"

Step-By-Step

1 If you are adding the gazebo to an existing deck, first remove the boards that would sit under the gazebo. Mark the locations of the five posts. Dig 12-inch-diameter holes, and pour concrete footings for the posts. Set a metal post anchor into each footing, and allow the concrete to cure. Cut the posts to length, adjust them for plumb, and attach them to the anchors with galvanized screws. Replace the decking, cutting the boards to fit tightly around the posts. If the gazebo is part of a new deck plan, fasten the posts to the fortified under-structure with ½-inch-diameter galvanized carriage bolts.

2 Cut the 4-by-6 beams so they span the distance from post to post. Wherever two beams meet, fasten them together with metal framing anchors.

3 Cut the 2-by-4 roof rafters to size. Notch each one with a bird's-mouth cut where it rests on top of a beam. Space the rafters 24 inches on center, and fasten them with 8d galvanized finishing nails. Bevel the top edges of the hip rafters at the corners of the gazebo's roof to a 45-degree angle to accept the 2-by-2 slats.

4 Cut 2 by 4s for the fascia. Bevel the top edges of the boards to 45 degrees, and then nail them to the ends of the rafter tails. Run the 2-by-4 fascia around the entire roof frame.

5 Install the 2 by 2s across the rafters, starting near the fascia and working up the roof. Cut miter joints at the corners, and fasten the 2 by 2s with 10d galvanized finishing nails.

6 From 2-by-8 stock, cut the 10 diagonal knee braces that fasten into the corners formed by the posts and beams. Create the decorative scroll-cut pattern with a saber saw or band saw (use the first piece as a template for marking up the others). Adhere the braces to the beams and posts with 3-inch decking screws.

7 Build the bench frame out of 2 by 6s, and screw it to the posts. Cut prefabricated lattice panels into 12-inch-wide strips, and sandwich them between 2-by-2 cleats nailed to the bench frame.

8 Cover the upper edge of the lattice panels with 2 by 6s to create the railing along the tops of the benches. Carefully notch the 2 by 6s so that they fit snugly around the posts.

9 Cut 2 by 6s for the bench seats. Note that the boards meet in the corner at a 45-degree angle. Fasten the boards with 10d galvanized finishing nails, leaving a 1/8-inch space between each one. Tap the nailheads well below the surface with a hammer and nailset.

10 Use an orbital sander to round all of the sharp corners and smooth all surfaces. Pay particular attention to the areas around the benches, railings, and posts. Finally, wipe off the dust, and apply a stain-blocking sealer and one or two coats of outdoor paint.

Corner Gazebo Bench Materials Checklist

- 4x4 posts
- 4x6 beams
- 2x4 rafters & fascia
- Prefabricated lattice panels
- 2x2 trellis stock
- 2x6 bench framing
- 2x8 braces
- Galvanized nails & outdoor screws
- Metal post anchors
- Metal framing brackets & fasteners
- Sanding & finishing supplies

Arbor Bench

This handsome, freestanding 5-foot-long arbor bench has five main sections: the two sides, the trellis top, the bench seat, and the backrest. The trellis top, which consists of two pairs of horizontal 2 by 6s and also seven 2-by-3 crosspieces, is fabricated piece by piece.

The structure has a number of subtle features that add to its appearance, strength, and comfort. It is designed so that no nail- or screwheads show, and copper-pipe end caps mask countersunk carriage bolts. A deep seat and angled backrest make the structure sturdy while providing comfort. The lattice side panels and overhead trellis are fashioned to train and support vines.

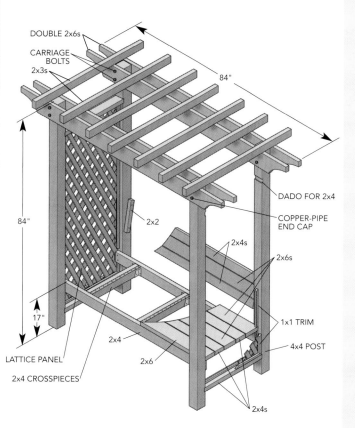

DOUBLE 2x6s
CARRIAGE BOLTS
2x3s
84"
DADO FOR 2x4
COPPER-PIPE END CAP
2x2
2x4s
2x6s
84"
1x1 TRIM
17"
4x4 POST
2x4
LATTICE PANEL
2x6
2x4 CROSSPIECES
2x4s

Designer's Sketchbook

Project | Open-Air Gazebo

A backyard sundeck offers a peaceful, private place to enjoy fresh air and sunshine. But even the most ardent sun worshiper needs a little shade every now and then. In addition to providing some cool shade, even in the midday sun, this open-air gazebo lends visual interest to the deck. Architect: Jean-Claude Hurni

Design Details

This gazebo measures just 8 by 8 feet at its base, so it is an easy fit for even the most modest-sized deck or patio. Four 4-by-4 posts support a hip roof comprising mostly 2 by 6s with a perimeter beam of double 2 by 8s. Along the lower edge of the roof is a series of cantilevered rafter tails with a decorative ogee profile. Three 2-by-2 lattice strips are fastened to the tops of the rafter tails to create a distinctive shadow pattern around the perimeter—and they're also handy for hanging potted plants.

Each of the four support posts and the short 4 by 4 at the roof peak are topped with decorative wood finials.

Building Notes

Each of the four 4-by-4 posts passes through the decking and sits on top of a concrete pier. The pier holes must be dug down to the frost line or a minimum of 18 inches.

The posts are attached to the concrete piers with rebar pins. The pins are inserted into each pier, the bottom of each post is bored with a hole, and once the concrete has cured, the posts are slipped over the pins.

If you are adding the gazebo to an existing deck, check local building codes. You might be allowed to attach the posts to the deck's floor joists with galvanized carriage bolts.

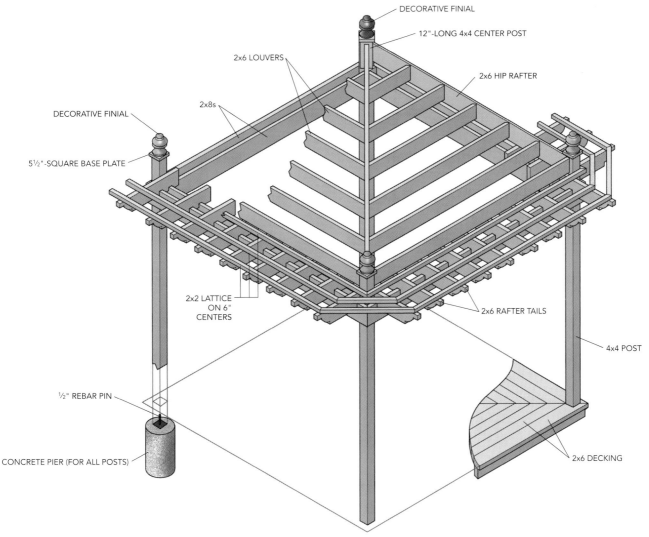

DECORATIVE FINIAL

12"-LONG 4x4 CENTER POST

2x6 LOUVERS

2x6 HIP RAFTER

2x8s

DECORATIVE FINIAL

5½"-SQUARE BASE PLATE

2x2 LATTICE ON 6" CENTERS

2x6 RAFTER TAILS

4x4 POST

½" REBAR PIN

CONCRETE PIER (FOR ALL POSTS)

2x6 DECKING

Casting just enough shade to keep the deck dappled in soft sun and shadows, this gazebo's open, airy structure is inviting and not at all imposing.

Step-By-Step

1 Pour the four concrete piers, and insert ½-inch-diameter-by-12-inch-long metal reinforcing bars 8 inches down into the wet concrete. Allow the concrete to cure for at least 24 hours.

2 Apply a thick, circular bead of exterior-grade caulk around the pins. Then cut four 4-by-4-inch gaskets out of an asphalt roof shingle. Punch a ½-inch-diameter hole in the center of the gaskets, and slip them over the pins. Press the gaskets down against the concrete piers, and then apply another circular bead of caulk to the tops of the gaskets. Bore a ½-inch-diameter-by-4-inch-deep hole in the bottom of each of the posts and slip the posts over the pins. Plumb each post with a 4-foot level to ensure they are perfectly vertical, and then attach the posts to a floor joist with long lag screws or carriage bolts.

3 Cut to length the eight 2-by-8 horizontal beams that run along the outside and inside of the posts. Fasten the beams to the posts with galvanized carriage bolts.

4 Cut the 21 rafter tails from 2-by-6 stock to 28 inches long. Using a saber saw, form the decorative ogee profile at one end of each piece.

5 With a portable circular saw, cut the 1½-inch-deep-by-6½-inch-wide notches that allow the rafter tails to fit over the beams. Start each of the notches 5 inches from the square end of the rafter tails, leaving 16½ inches of each tail canti-levered over the edge of the outer beams. Space the rafter tails 12 inches on center, bore pilot holes, and fasten the rafters to the beams with 2½-inch decking screws.

6 Cut the four hip rafters out of 2 by 6s, and install them with the aid of a helper. Each rafter runs from a corner post up to the peak of the 12-inch-long center post. Secure the rafters with 2½-inch decking screws driven into the corner posts and center post.

7 Next, install the series of tiered 2-by-6 louvers that start at the base of the roof, near the top of the four corner posts, and continue all the way up to the peak. Six 2-by-6 louvers, spaced 6 inches on center, are required for each of the four sides of the roof. Miter-cut the ends of the boards to an angle of 45 degrees, and then screw the boards to the rafters.

8 Cut 2 by 2s to length to create the lattice strips for the tops of the rafter tails. Space the strips 6 inches on center, and secure them with 3-inch decking screws. At the corners, where the 2 by 2s form a 45-degree angle, miter-cut the ends of the strips to 22½ degrees. Be sure each miter joint falls directly on a rafter tail.

9 Finish the top of the four corner posts and the short post at the peak with a base plate and finial. Cut the 5½-inch-square base plates from a 1-by-6 board. Fasten them to the tops of the posts with exterior-grade caulk and 8d galvanized finishing nails. Bore a center hole for the finials' mounting screws, and then screw the finials to the posts.

10 Paint or stain the gazebo, as desired. (You may want to accomplish this before you assemble the structure.) If you choose not to apply a paint or stain, brush on a coat of clear wood preservative to protect the gazebo from the harmful effects of sun and moisture.

Plan View

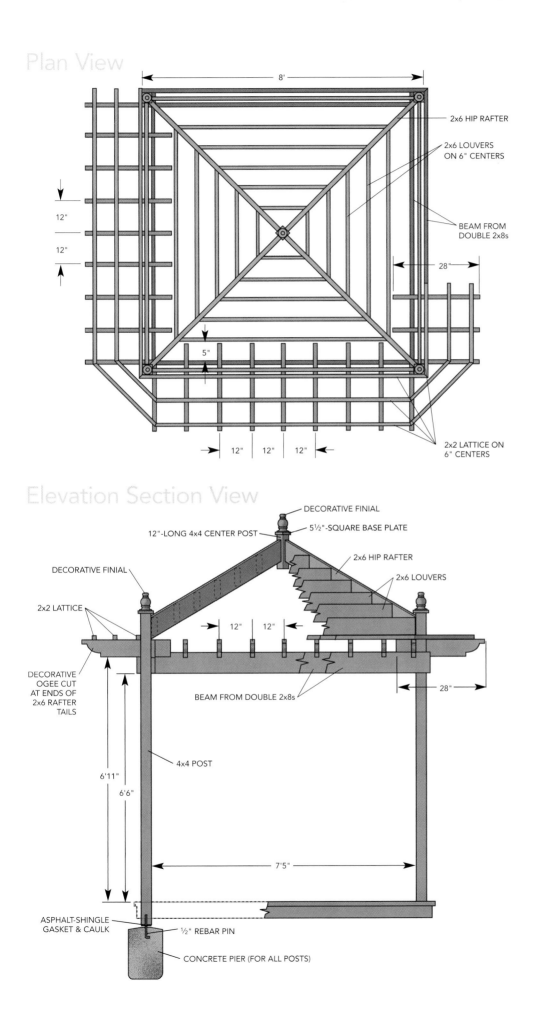

8'

2x6 HIP RAFTER

2x6 LOUVERS ON 6" CENTERS

BEAM FROM DOUBLE 2x8s

12"

12"

28"

5"

12" 12" 12"

2x2 LATTICE ON 6" CENTERS

Elevation Section View

DECORATIVE FINIAL

12"-LONG 4x4 CENTER POST

5½"-SQUARE BASE PLATE

2x6 HIP RAFTER

2x6 LOUVERS

DECORATIVE FINIAL

2x2 LATTICE

12" 12"

DECORATIVE OGEE CUT AT ENDS OF 2x6 RAFTER TAILS

BEAM FROM DOUBLE 2x8s

28"

4x4 POST

6'11"

6'6"

7'5"

ASPHALT-SHINGLE GASKET & CAULK

½" REBAR PIN

CONCRETE PIER (FOR ALL POSTS)

Open-Air Gazebo Materials Checklist

- Concrete & #4 rebar for footings
- 4x4 posts
- 2x8 beams
- 2x6 louvers, rafters & rafter tails
- 2x2 trellis stock
- 1x6 for base plates
- Caulking compound
- Asphalt roof shingles
- Galvanized nails & outdoor screws
- Galvanized lag screws & washers
- Galvanized carriage bolts
- Metal post anchors or rebar pins
- Decorative wood finials
- Sanding & finishing supplies
- Exterior primer
- Paint, stain, or wood preservative

Party Pavilion

Cozy enough for just one or two yet with plenty of room for a small crowd, this 12-foot-square gazebo-like pavilion sports a deck, benches, and a lath-style roof.

Four posts at each corner rise from the foundation to support the deck, benches, and roof framing. Four ridge beams run from one post at each corner to a 4-by-4 hub, beveled and turned at a 45-degree angle, at the center. The upper edges of the beams are also beveled to receive spaced 1-by-2 roofing.

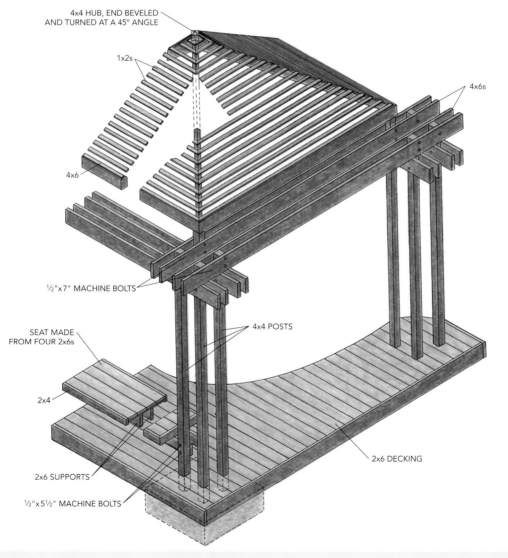

4x4 HUB, END BEVELED AND TURNED AT A 45° ANGLE

1x2s

4x6s

4x6

½"x7" MACHINE BOLTS

SEAT MADE FROM FOUR 2x6s

4x4 POSTS

2x4

2x6 DECKING

2x6 SUPPORTS

½"x5½" MACHINE BOLTS

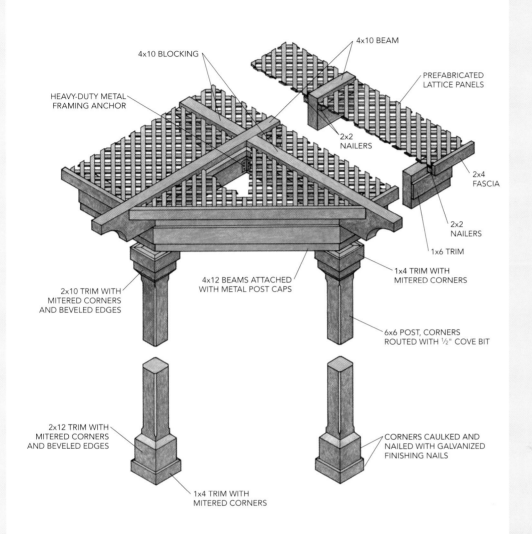

4x10 BLOCKING

4x10 BEAM

PREFABRICATED
LATTICE PANELS

HEAVY-DUTY METAL
FRAMING ANCHOR

2x2
NAILERS

2x4
FASCIA

2x2
NAILERS

1x6 TRIM

1x4 TRIM WITH
MITERED CORNERS

2x10 TRIM WITH
MITERED CORNERS
AND BEVELED EDGES

4x12 BEAMS ATTACHED
WITH METAL POST CAPS

6x6 POST, CORNERS
ROUTED WITH ½" COVE BIT

2x12 TRIM WITH
MITERED CORNERS
AND BEVELED EDGES

CORNERS CAULKED AND
NAILED WITH GALVANIZED
FINISHING NAILS

1x4 TRIM WITH
MITERED CORNERS

Dining Octagon

Conforming to the contours of an eight-sided brick patio, this handsome pavilion creates a formal outdoor dining space. Both the octagonal shape and the careful detailing of posts and beams contribute to the overhead's feeling of formality.

The 6-by-6 posts gain plenty of visual interest from nailed-on, mitered trim. Around the perimeter, 4-by-12 beams, mitered at the ends as well, rest on the posts. The beams are trimmed with a continuous 2-by-4 fascia. Three 4-by-10 beams run from one end to the other; matching 4 by 10s that are fastened with framing anchors butt into them and provide blocking between them. Diagonal-patterned prefabricated lattice panels are secured to 2-by-2 nailers.

Project | Contemporary Trellis

This 13-foot-wide by 12-foot-long shade trellis extends over a multilevel deck, shedding filtered light on the outdoor space and into the house through sliding doors. It is painted to match the home's trim and the deck railings.
Designer/Builder: Henry Angeli

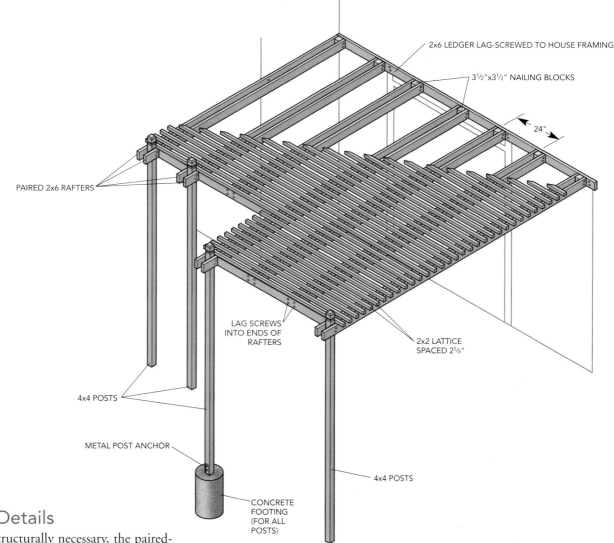

2x6 LEDGER LAG-SCREWED TO HOUSE FRAMING

3½"x3½" NAILING BLOCKS

24"

PAIRED 2x6 RAFTERS

LAG SCREWS INTO ENDS OF RAFTERS

2x2 LATTICE SPACED 2⅝"

4x4 POSTS

METAL POST ANCHOR

4x4 POSTS

CONCRETE FOOTING (FOR ALL POSTS)

Design Details

While not structurally necessary, the paired-rafter detail adds interest to the design, as do the routed channel and chamfer features that are at the post tops. Nailing blocks between the rafter pairs enable very solid connections without the need for utilitarian joist hangers.

Painting the trellis to match the trim and deck railings integrates the structure with the home and deck. While this trellis is designed to extend over a second, grade-level deck and the yard, the easily adapted design could be stepped or angled to conform to the shape of any deck.

Redwood is a smart choice because it accepts and holds a painted finish much better than does pressure-treated lumber. In order to prevent stains from natural resins, especially noticeable through white or light-colored paint, use an oil-based primer to seal the wood. Premium-quality 100 percent acrylic-latex exterior paint is the best topcoat.

Building Notes

Although this trellis was designed and built by an accomplished furniture maker, the structure is very easy to construct. The use of post anchors makes it easy to cut the posts precisely. The 2 by 2s for the trellis are cut with a table saw from 2-by-4 stock to save on the high price of 2-by-2 redwood.

To guide the positioning of the 2 by 2s for a uniform overhang, rip a 2 by 4 to the overhang dimension and clamp it to the outside of the end rafters. Then start installing the 2 by 2s at the outer edge, and work toward the house. Make a couple of U-shape jigs to hang over the rafters, and set the desired spacing. As you near the house, check the remaining space against the 2 by 2s left. Make adjustments so the last one does not fall too close or too far from the house.

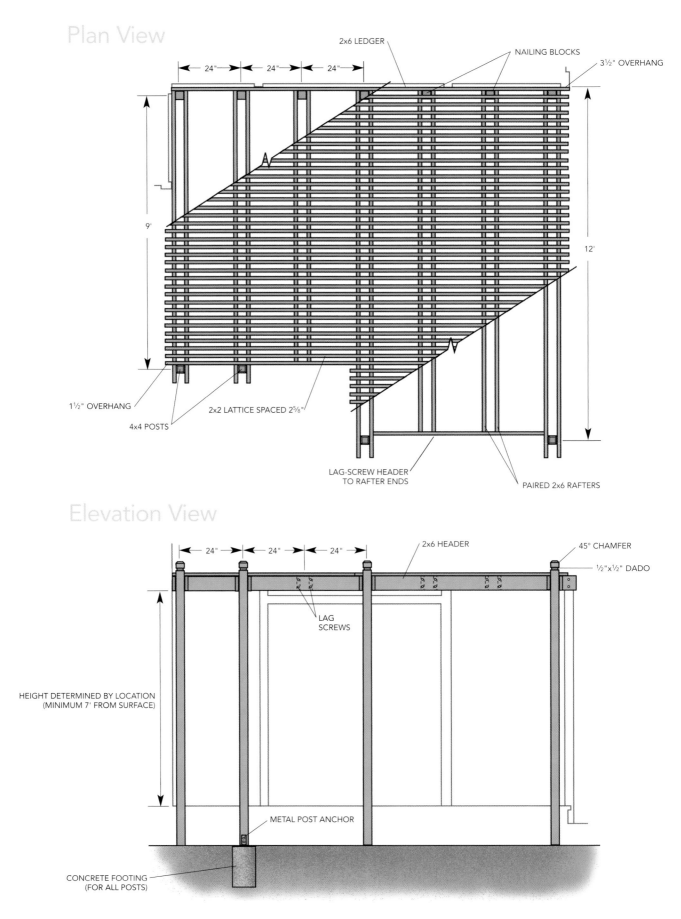

Plan View

2x6 LEDGER

NAILING BLOCKS

3½" OVERHANG

24"　24"　24"

9'

12'

1½" OVERHANG

4x4 POSTS

2x2 LATTICE SPACED 2⅝"

LAG-SCREW HEADER TO RAFTER ENDS

PAIRED 2x6 RAFTERS

Elevation View

24"　24"　24"

2x6 HEADER

45° CHAMFER

½"x½" DADO

LAG SCREWS

HEIGHT DETERMINED BY LOCATION (MINIMUM 7' FROM SURFACE)

METAL POST ANCHOR

CONCRETE FOOTING (FOR ALL POSTS)

Step-By-Step

1 Locate the post positions by measuring and squaring off from the house. Dig holes that extend 6 inches below your area's frost line or at least 12 inches deep. Pour the footings, and embed post anchors for 4 by 4s in concrete.

2 Cut the ledger, and attach nailing blocks with ⁵/₁₆-by-3-inch lag screws. Then bolt the ledger to the house framing. Methods vary widely depending on a house's siding type as well as the location of the framing. Consult your local building department for specifications in your area.

3 Position the posts on post anchors. Drill clearance holes for ³/₈-by-5-inch carriage bolts. Using both a spirit level and a long straightedge or a water level, mark a point on each post that is level with the bottom of the ledger.

4 Remove the posts, and cut their tops 9½ inches above the marks. Then cut a ½-by-½-inch dado around the posts using either a router or a circular saw and chisel. Chamfer the top ½ inch of each post at a 45-degree angle. Reinstall the posts, and brace them plumb.

5 Cut the rafters that attach to the posts to length. Bore clearance holes through the rafters, and drill pilot holes into the post and nailing blocks at the ledger. Attach the rafters to the insides of the posts with ⁵/₁₆-by-3-inch lag screws and washers and to the ledger with ⁵/₁₆-by-3½-inch carriage bolts, washers, and nuts.

6 Cut the header between the installed rafters to length. Predrill clearance holes through the joists. Clamp or otherwise support the header while you drill pilot holes for two ⁵/₁₆-by-3-inch lag screws. Then install the header with the lag screws and washers.

7 Measure and cut all the rafters that fit between the ledger and header, and saturate the ends with wood preservative. When the rafters are completely dry, attach them to the nailing blocks at the ledger and the header with lag screws following the directions in Step 5.

8 Using a table saw, rip enough 2-by-4 stock for all the 1½-by-1½-inch trellis cross members (or use 2-by-2 stock), and cut them to length. Remove the saw marks with a jointer or surface planer; otherwise, install the cross members cut side up.

9 Sand the trellis cross members, and then saturate both exposed ends with wood preservative. Apply an oil-based primer, and then finish with a 100 percent acrylic-latex exterior paint.

10 Nail a temporary brace across the tops of the two outer rafters to hold them parallel. Install the 2 by 2s with 3½-inch deck screws, using wood blocks to set both the overhang and the space in between the members.

Contemporary Trellis Materials Checklist

- Concrete & #4 rebar for footing
- Nailing blocks
- 4x4 posts
- 2x6 rafters & ledger
- 2x2 trellis stock
- Galvanized nails & outdoor screws
- Galvanized lag screws & washers
- Galvanized carriage bolts, washers & nuts
- Metal post anchors
- Sanding & finishing supplies
- Wood preservative
- Exterior primer
- Acrylic-latex exterior paint

Modern Elegance

Attached to the house at only one corner, this patio roof's boxy lines and detailing complement the home's contemporary architecture. The structure is an egg-crate formation of 4-by-8 and 4-by-10 beams, mounted on 6-by-6 redwood posts. Its charm results from the built-up trim—1-by and 2-by stock that has been mitered, beveled, and nailed to the posts and beams. False partial posts attach to the house walls to complete the theme. Roofing of 3 by 3s, spaced on 10-inch centers, allows more sun than shade.

All seams and joints are caulked to minimize any warping or moisture damage. The wood, which is surfaced Douglas fir except for the posts, is painted to blend with the house trim.

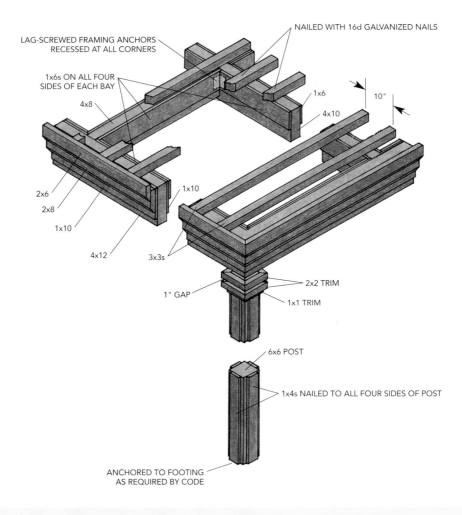

NAILED WITH 16d GALVANIZED NAILS

LAG-SCREWED FRAMING ANCHORS
RECESSED AT ALL CORNERS

1x6s ON ALL FOUR
SIDES OF EACH BAY

4x8

1x6

4x10

10"

2x6

2x8

1x10

1x10

4x12

3x3s

1" GAP

2x2 TRIM

1x1 TRIM

6x6 POST

1x4s NAILED TO ALL FOUR SIDES OF POST

ANCHORED TO FOOTING
AS REQUIRED BY CODE

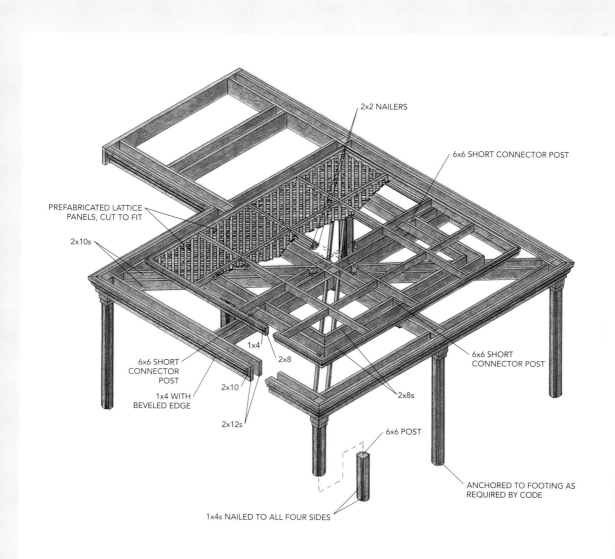

2x2 NAILERS

6x6 SHORT CONNECTOR POST

PREFABRICATED LATTICE PANELS, CUT TO FIT

2x10s

1x4

2x8

6x6 SHORT CONNECTOR POST

1x4 WITH BEVELED EDGE

2x10

2x12s

6x6 SHORT CONNECTOR POST

2x8s

6x6 POST

ANCHORED TO FOOTING AS REQUIRED BY CODE

1x4s NAILED TO ALL FOUR SIDES

Patio Pavilion

The elegance of this structure comes partially from its posts and beams—they are clad with built-up trim, some of it beveled and mitered—and partially from its overall design. The beams converge at the center, making the roof quite an eye-catcher.

Unlike most house-attached patio roofs, this shelter is linked to the house only by a pair of beams. The overhead's shape reflects that of the patio below it.

Beneath the light-toned stain is resawn Douglas fir (the posts are decay-resistant redwood). All joints were carefully caulked to keep moisture out.

Project | Garden Retreat

Softened by outdoor fabric that billows in the breeze, this bold retreat is a dramatic focal point in an elegantly landscaped garden. The structure is quite simple in form: just four columns that support a rectangle of hefty beams and rafters. But the real beauty lies in the details. Designed to echo the home's Monterey Colonial architecture, the posts have squared-off lines and beam ends are articulated with profiles found in the house's architectural mouldings.
Courtesy of Pasadena Showcase House 2006. Design: C & K Landscape Design

Design Details

Four 8-foot fiberglass-reinforced polymer columns support the structure's four corners. These stand on concrete footings. To give the unit lateral stability and also lock it down to the foundation, 1-inch grade A307 threaded rods are embedded in the footings and extended up through the hollow columns and into holes bored in the beams. The rods are cinched tight with washers and nuts. Be sure to follow the column manufacturer's specifications for this type of anchor.

The columns are white and do not require a finish for protection. The rest of the structure is painted white to match. The curtains are made from sheer synthetic mesh, which holds up well outdoors. If you intend to have the curtains made by a professional, order them before you begin construction.

Building Notes

Because the overhead is built from just a few large components, construction is relatively simple but heavy work. You will need a couple of helpers, and you may need to rent a few tools, including a portable band saw, for cutting the curved patterns at the ends of the beams and rafters, and a ½-inch power drill and long drill bit (or an extension shaft), for drilling holes through the beams.

You can precut all the rafters before assembling them. To ensure that all of the rafters match one another, lay out and cut the end detail on one of them, and then use this rafter as a pattern for marking and cutting the others.

Apply a coat of primer and a topcoat to all wooden components and the beam hanger brackets before assembly, and then touch them up when the structure is completed.

Garden Retreat Materials Checklist

- Concrete & #4 rebar for footings
- 1-inch grade A307 threaded rods & coupler nuts
- Washers & nuts
- Fiberglass-reinforced polymer columns
- Beam hangers
- 4x12 beams
- 4x6 rafters
- Galvanized nails
- Wood primer & paint
- Sanding & finishing supplies
- Curtains

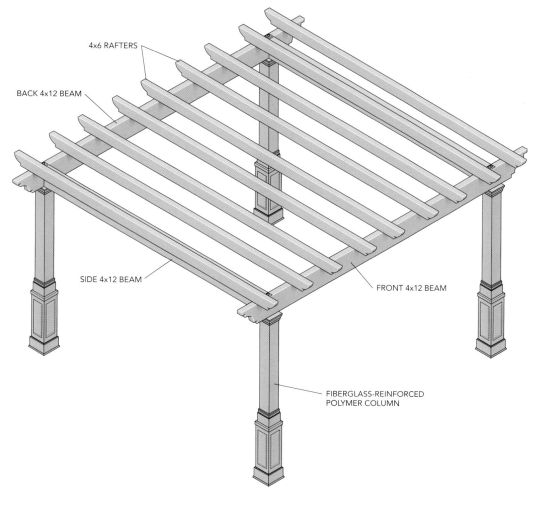

4x6 RAFTERS

BACK 4x12 BEAM

SIDE 4x12 BEAM

FRONT 4x12 BEAM

FIBERGLASS-REINFORCED POLYMER COLUMN

Step-By-Step

1 Lay out and pour the footings according to the plan view below and the techniques discussed on pages 65–66. Be sure their surfaces are level with one another.

2 Before the concrete sets up, embed a 2-foot length of 1-inch grade A307 threaded rod into the center of each footing so it is plumb and protrudes 4 inches above the surface; thread a coupler nut onto the top of each rod. Check the measurements between the rods. Allow the concrete to cure.

3 Assemble the columns according to the manufacturer's instructions, and set them over the threaded rods on each footing. Once the base of each column is in place, slide a 9-foot-long threaded rod into the column's hollow center. Lift the column onto blocks, and couple the long rod to the short one. Remove the blocks.

4 Cut the 16-foot-long front and back 4-by-12 beams to length. Use a compass and a square to mark a pattern for the detail at the end of one beam. To cut a curve, you will need to use a portable band saw. (You can modify the pattern to include only straight cuts that can be made with a power saw and handsaw.) Use the first end that you cut as a pattern for marking the other three ends.

5 Double-check the distance between the long threaded rods that protrude above the columns, and then bore centered ¾-inch-diameter holes through one beam to receive the rods.

6 With two or three sturdy ladders and a couple of strong helpers, lift the beam up onto the columns and slide it down over the rods. Repeat with the other long beam. Use a level to make sure each beam is level and that the beams are level with each other. You can make small adjustments by tapping cedar shims between a beam and a column.

7 Paint 4-inch beam hanger brackets white, and, using only approved galvanized nails, mount them, centered on each column, on the inner faces of the long beams. Measure the distances between brackets from beam to beam, and cut the side beams to these lengths. Prime and paint the cut ends, and allow the paint to dry. Then lift these beams up into the

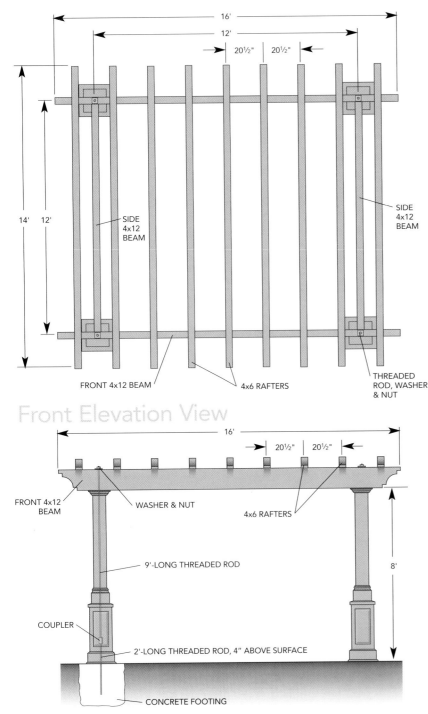

Plan View

16'
12'
20½" 20½"
14' 12'
SIDE 4x12 BEAM
SIDE 4x12 BEAM
FRONT 4x12 BEAM
4x6 RAFTERS
THREADED ROD, WASHER & NUT

Front Elevation View

16'
20½" 20½"
FRONT 4x12 BEAM
WASHER & NUT
4x6 RAFTERS
9'-LONG THREADED ROD
8'
COUPLER
2'-LONG THREADED ROD, 4" ABOVE SURFACE
CONCRETE FOOTING

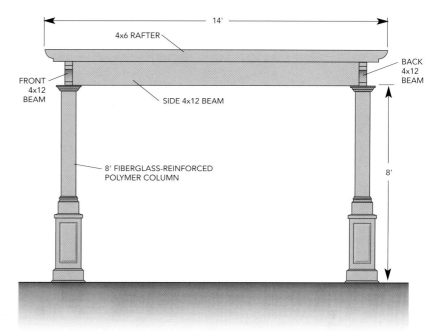

14'

4x6 RAFTER

FRONT
4x12
BEAM

BACK
4x12
BEAM

SIDE 4x12 BEAM

8'

8' FIBERGLASS-REINFORCED
POLYMER COLUMN

brackets, and secure them using galvanized nails approved for the hangers.

8 Mark the tops of the 16-foot-long beams for placement of the 14-foot-long 4-by-6 rafters on 21½-inch centers. Lift the precut and painted rafters up onto the long beams, and set the first one in place at the center marks so that the overhang is equal on both ends. Toenail the rafter to each beam with two 16d galvanized nails on each side. Repeat with the remaining rafters, working from the center outward.

9 Prime any raw wood and touch up the structure with paint where necessary.

10 After the paint dries, affix the curtain rods and then hang the curtains.

Classic Revival

A cross between post-modern architecture and a Greco-Roman temple, this pavilion offers a dramatic outdoor setting.

Beneath the stuccoed exterior of each post is a pressure-treated 4 by 4, anchored to the concrete patio and footing with a metal post anchor. Short 2 by 4s radiate from the center post to form a framework for the stucco. The 2-by-12 beams are bolted to the posts; intermediate 2 by 10s are bolted to the inner beams.

Above, a layer of 2 by 2s on 12-inch centers crisscrosses a second layer. The top is wrapped with 2 by 4s, mitered at the corners.

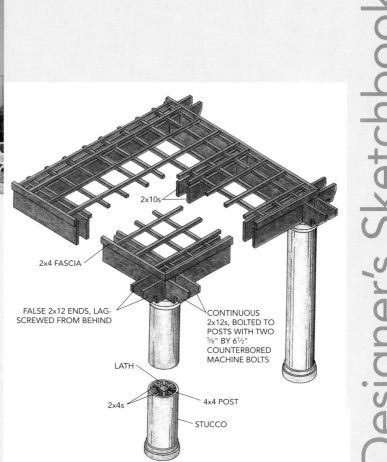

2x10s

2x4 FASCIA

FALSE 2x12 ENDS, LAG-
SCREWED FROM BEHIND

CONTINUOUS
2x12s, BOLTED TO
POSTS WITH TWO
⅝" BY 6½"
COUNTERBORED
MACHINE BOLTS

LATH

2x4s

4x4 POST

STUCCO

Designer's Sketchbook

A pair of 28-inch-long benches flanks the 36-inch-wide passageway through this garden bower. The painted portal provides a place for peaceful contemplation, private conversation, or a relaxing break from garden work. Design: Elizabeth Lair

Design Details

The designer's choice of primarily 1-by lumber (mostly 1 by 2s) for this structure, rather than an equal mix of 1-by and 2-by lumber, simplifies construction and keeps materials costs down without compromising sturdiness.

The design is easily adapted for wider paths, as is the profile of the arch that supports the roof trellis.

The ladder-like design of the sides, back, and roof also make the bower a perfect vehicle for training and supporting climbing plants and vines (see "Vines for Patio Roofs and Gazebos" on page 152 for a list of the most popular and hardy varieties).

Because the bower is exposed to frequent garden waterings, a wood preservative was applied before construction and all end grain was thoroughly soaked. The members were then carefully primed and painted to prevent the peeling and cracking that leads to total paint failure and wood rot.

Building Notes

The completed structure is lightweight, so subassemblies or even the entire piece can be built offsite. Precut all parts for efficiency; to reduce the risk of error; and to allow for all pieces to be treated with a wood preservative, primed, and painted prior to assembly.

To make sure that the left and right sides of the arch, which must be drawn freehand, are mirror images, create a ¼-inch plywood template for one half, trace it onto your stock, and then flip it over and trace it onto the other half. Use this first arch as a template for the second one.

Before cutting the strips for the diamonds, cut a couple to verify that they will work in all the locations. To prevent splitting the wood, bore pilot holes wherever screws are within 2 inches of the end of a board.

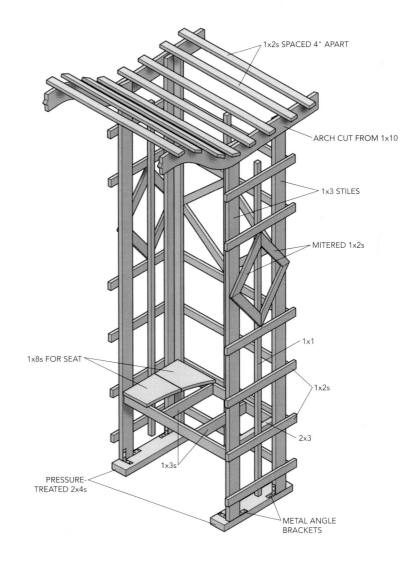

1x2s SPACED 4" APART

ARCH CUT FROM 1x10

1x3 STILES

MITERED 1x2s

1x1

1x2s

2x3

1x8s FOR SEAT

1x3s

PRESSURE-TREATED 2x4s

METAL ANGLE BRACKETS

Elevation View

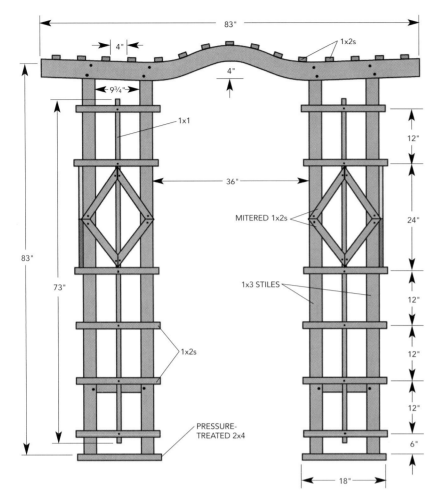

Side Elevation View

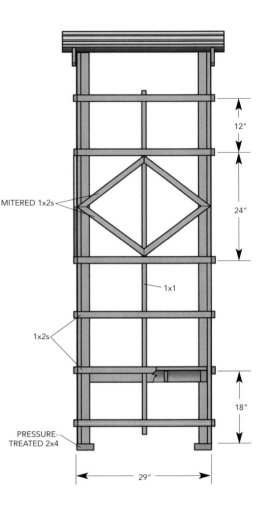

Garden Bower Materials Checklist

- 2x4 pressure-treated sills
- 1x1s
- 1x2 trellis stock
- 1x3s
- 1x8s
- 1x10s
- 2x3s
- ¼-inch plywood (for template)
- Galvanized nails & outdoor screws
- Metal angle brackets & screws
- Wood stakes
- Sanding & finishing supplies
- Paint, stain, or wood preservative

Step-By-Step

1 Cut all the parts, except the 1 by 2s for the diamonds. Cut the 1 by 2s: 20 at 18 inches, 12 at 29 inches, four at 12 inches, and 15 at 35 inches. Then cut the 1-by-10 stock for the arch to two 83-inch lengths.

2 Draw the arch on a piece of ¼-inch plywood, and then, using a jigsaw, cut it out to make a template. The 4-inch-wide arch rises to 4 inches in the center and to 1 inch at each end. To facilitate cutting, draw vertical lines where the curves begin or change direction at the center point and above each inside stile.

Plan View of Seat

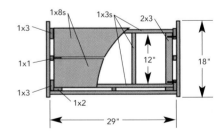

3 Soak the ends of all the pieces in a wood preservative that accepts paint. When the wood is completely dry, apply exterior primer to all surfaces and then a coat of paint. Apply a touch-up or final coat after assembly is completed.

4 Make four identical ladder trellises. Drive 1¼-inch exterior screws through the 83-inch verticals into the backs of the 18-inch horizontals, and then drive nails through the horizontals into the 73-inch center braces.

5 To determine the cuts for the pieces forming the diamonds, mark the vertical center on the rungs and then mark the horizontal center between the rungs on the stiles. Hold a length of 1 by 2 in place, and mark the angles. Secure the diamonds with nails after preserving, priming, and painting them.

6 Lay a pair of trellises flat on their outside faces, 36 inches apart, parallel to each other and with their ends aligned against a straightedge. Place an arch into position, centered under the trellis stiles, and then secure it with two screws at each stile. Repeat for the other pair of trellises.

7 Secure the 83-inch 1-by-3 stiles to the trellis assemblies with nails spaced every 8 inches. Assemble the support framework for the bench by nailing each 12-inch rung on edge between the 29-inch rails.

8 Nail two trellises together with five horizontal braces attached to the stiles. Attach the seat framework between them 18 inches up from the base with 2½-inch screws driven through the trellis faces and into the ends of the framework. Repeat the procedure with the other two trellises.

9 Lay the assemblies onto their sides, elevated a few inches to allow for the 2-inch overhang, and secure the top trellis members onto the arch supports with nails. Start at the center and work outward, using a wood block to ensure uniform 4-inch spacing.

10 Attach pressure-treated 2-by-4 feet onto the legs with metal angle brackets. Level the ground, and stand the trellis up to install the back center support and the benches on either side. Attach the feet to stakes driven into the ground. Then cut off the stakes flush with the top of the feet.

Inviting Entry

Arbors can create magic at a home's entry. Often combined with a fence and gate, an entry arbor is a mood setter and a dramatic way of welcoming guests. Arbors can also function to create shade or shelter, as well as provide structural support for gateposts.

This arching entry arbor not only invites guests to the front door but also creates a sense of place. The arch is built from a double thickness of 2 by 12s cut into arcs and then nailed together. Joints are staggered between front and back sections. The arch was sanded, caulked, and painted to hide joints. The sides are prefabricated lattice panels cut to fit the framing.

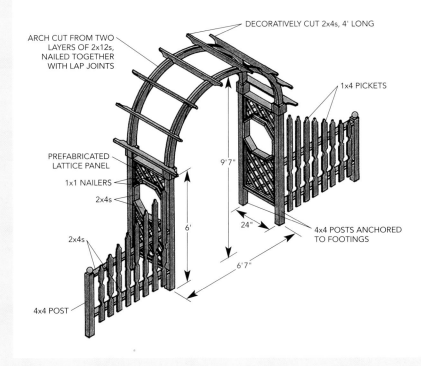

ARCH CUT FROM TWO LAYERS OF 2x12s, NAILED TOGETHER WITH LAP JOINTS

DECORATIVELY CUT 2x4s, 4' LONG

1x4 PICKETS

PREFABRICATED LATTICE PANEL

1x1 NAILERS

2x4s

9'7"

6'

24"

4x4 POSTS ANCHORED TO FOOTINGS

2x4s

6'7"

4x4 POST

Vines for Patio Roofs & Gazebos

For many homeowners, an overhead or gazebo is not just a way to provide shade or shelter; it is a means to enhance the garden, as well. Climbing vines are an integral consideration in many designs, providing color, lush foliage, fragrance, and shade seasonally or year-round, depending on where you live.

If such is your desire, your plan could include a watering system that will meet the needs of your plantings yet not deliver water directly to a wood structure. Even so, all posts and beams should be well treated with a wood preservative to prevent moisture damage.

Following is a list of some of the hardiest vines, by their common names and scientific names (if different) and the minimum temperatures that the plants will endure in winter.

Anemone clematis (*Clematis montana*; −10°F) This deciduous, fast-growing vine showcases white to pink flowers in early spring before its leaves emerge. A vigorous climber, its light-green leaves provide moderate to dense shade. It requires light pruning.

Blood-red trumpet vine (*Distictis buccinatoria*; 24°F) A rapidly growing evergreen vine, this plant blooms brilliantly when the weather is warm; its trumpet-shaped flowers are orange-red fading to bluish red. It provides moderate shade.

Bougainvillea (30°F) Though the peak flowering period comes in summer, blooms—in dazzlingly bright colors of purple, magenta, crimson, brick red, orange, yellow, pink, or white—may appear from spring through autumn and even into winter in the mildest climates. A fast, vigorous grower with medium-green leaves, this evergreen supplies moderate to dense shade.

Clematis jackmanii (−20°F) Though it provides only very light shade, this vine is prized for its large purple flowers, which emerge in summer. Dormant stems must be cut back when new growth starts in the spring.

Common white jasmine (*Jasminum officinale*; 5°F) This rapidly growing evergreen vine loses some of its foliage in colder regions. Fragrant white flowers bloom throughout the spring. After blooming, the vine must be thinned and pruned to maintain its attractiveness.

Evergreen clematis (*Clematis armandii*; 0°F) A slow starter, evergreen clematis grows rapidly in warm weather and provides light to moderate shade. It has glossy dark-green foliage that droops downward, creating a strongly textured pattern; flowers, which appear in spring, are fragrant, white, and shaped like stars. After blooming, the plant must be pruned to keep it in check.

Giant Burmese honeysuckle (*Lonicera hildebrandiana*; 20°F) The dark-green leaves of this plant provide moderate shade. Fragrant flowers up to 7 inches long bloom in summer. They are white when they first open, and then turn yellow and soft orange as they age.

Grapes (American, −25°F; European, 10°F) The luxuriant foliage of this deciduous and rapidly growing vine produces dense, cool shade. Fruiting varieties yield edible grapes but may also attract insects.

Roses (0°F) Vining roses provide light to moderate amounts of shade and usually grow rapidly. Many varieties are available; choose disease-resistant types with foliage that does not easily mildew.

Sweet autumn clematis (*Clematis dioscoreifolia robusta*; −10°F) From late summer into autumn, this deciduous vine offers frothy masses of small, fragrant creamy-white flowers and glossy dark-green leaves. It grows quickly and provides moderate to heavy shade.

Wisteria (−30°F) Fragrant, pendulous clusters of white, pink, lavender, or purple flowers (pictured above) characterize this popular vine. The light-green foliage provides moderate to heavy shade.

Project Garden Room Gazebo

This crisp octagonal garden room is reminiscent of a classic Victorian gazebo, but it cuts a markedly modern profile. Simple yet effective trim frames the handsome reveals that create plays of light on the interior as the sun moves across the sky. The walls are open to breezes, and an acrylic-sheet skylight adds illumination inside.
Architect: Lou Kimball

Design Details

The octagonal shape of this structure is very efficient at creating maximum space within a minimum perimeter. The interior space provides a full 14 feet of unobstructed room from wall to wall—plenty of area for a table and chairs or other furniture.

The acrylic-sheet skylight can be located in any section of the roof. In warmer climates, facing it north will minimize heat build-up; in cooler areas, placing it toward the south will maximize warmth.

If desired, you can scale the room down, but if you scale it up, have a professional check that the lumber sizes are sufficient.

Building Notes

The garden room rests on a concrete grade-beam foundation and slab floor, which are subject to code. The beam must be at minimum 18 inches deep or descend to the frost line. Check your region's standards with your building department.

A great advantage of the framing method used is that seven of the eight wall sections are identical. You can measure the pieces for a single section, use them as templates for the others, and cut them all at one time. If you don't own a power miter saw, this project offers the perfect excuse for buying one—it will pay for itself in the labor it saves.

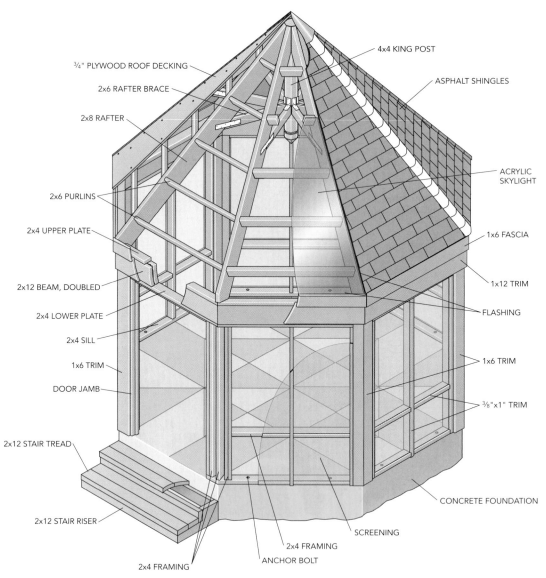

¾" PLYWOOD ROOF DECKING

2x6 RAFTER BRACE

2x8 RAFTER

2x6 PURLINS

2x4 UPPER PLATE

2x12 BEAM, DOUBLED

2x4 LOWER PLATE

2x4 SILL

1x6 TRIM

DOOR JAMB

2x12 STAIR TREAD

2x12 STAIR RISER

2x4 FRAMING

2x4 FRAMING

ANCHOR BOLT

SCREENING

4x4 KING POST

ASPHALT SHINGLES

ACRYLIC SKYLIGHT

1x6 FASCIA

1x12 TRIM

FLASHING

1x6 TRIM

³⁄₈"x1" TRIM

CONCRETE FOUNDATION

Step-By-Step

1 Locate and measure for the octagonal foundation, and then dig the foundation trench. Stake form boards around the trench to create a grade beam 18 inches high on the outside and exactly 14 feet, 7 inches from wall to wall. Each wall segment should measure 6 feet from corner to corner. Place, rake, and level a gravel bed 6 inches deep so that its top is 4 inches below the form boards. Add a layer of 6-mil vapor barrier, holding it in place with a few handfuls of gravel. Be careful not to perforate it.

2 Add reinforcing bar, and then pour the concrete. Screed the surface to create a ¼-inch-per-foot runoff slope from the center to the perimeter. Sink anchor bolts in the concrete everywhere except in the doorway. The slab floor of this garden room has a pattern of scored lines that crisscross on 2-foot centers. After smoothing the surface with a steel trowel, use a jointing tool to score the lines. Be sure to wait until the concrete is firm enough to support your weight while you kneel on top of long boards, which is the position you will take to score the surface. Cover the finished slab, and keep it damp for a day or two. Then strip the forms. If you wish, use concrete stain to color the slab once it has cured.

3 To build the seven identical wall sections, start by cutting the 22½-degree angles at the ends of each 6-foot pressure-treated lower plate. Cut two ¾-by-¾-inch slots on 2-foot centers across the bottom of each plate for drainage. With 16d nails, fasten pairs of 81-inch studs at each end of each plate, spacing them in from the ends to accept the angled bridging studs you will add later. Fasten a final stud in the center of each section, bracing it with horizontal 2 by 4s fastened with outdoor screws. Finish with a 2-by-4 upper plate. Measure and drill ½-inch holes in each bottom plate, and bolt each wall section to the foundation. Then, counterbore for the washers and nuts, and, using a hacksaw, cut the bolts so that they are flush with the plates. Connect the wall sections to each other using angled bridging studs that are screwed in place.

Top Plan

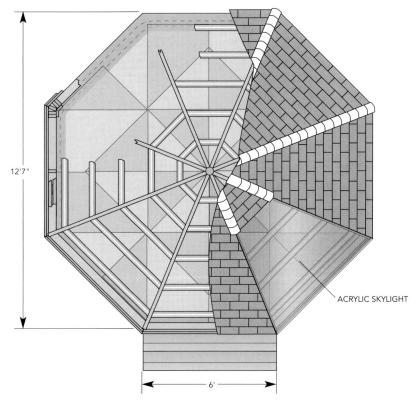

ACRYLIC SKYLIGHT

12'7"

6'

Front Elevation

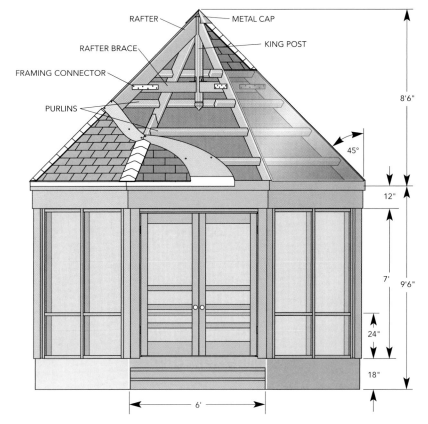

RAFTER   METAL CAP

RAFTER BRACE   KING POST

FRAMING CONNECTOR

PURLINS

8'6"

45°

12"

7'

9'6"

24"

18"

6'

Garden Room Gazebo Materials Checklist

- Gravel or crushed-rock fill
- 6-mil polyethylene vapor barrier
- #3 & #5 rebar
- Concrete
- 2-by-4 pressure-treated sills
- ½-inch anchor bolts, washers & nuts
- 2-by-4 framing & top plates
- 2-by-6 purlins & roof braces
- 2-by-8 rafters
- 2-by-12 headers & stair stringers & treads
- ½-inch exterior plywood spacers for headers
- ¾-inch exterior plywood roof decking
- 1-by-6 fascia
- ⅜-by-½-inch trim
- 1-by-4, 1-by-6 & 1-by-12 trim
- 4-by-4 king post
- Metal framing connectors & proprietary screws
- Door-jamb stock
- Pair 30-inch-by-7-foot screen doors
- Screening
- Galvanized nails
- 3½-inch outdoor screws
- Galvanized roofing nails
- Composition shingles
- Metal drip edge
- Acrylic-sheet panel & metal flashing
- Custom-made metal roof cap
- Silicone sealant
- Roofing cement
- Sanding & finishing supplies
- Paint, stain, or preservative

Foundation Detail

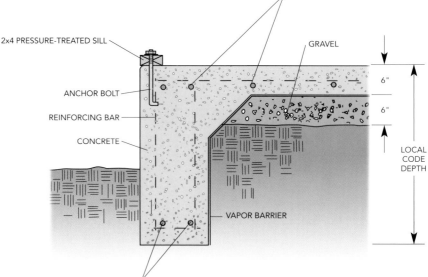

REINFORCING BAR

2x4 PRESSURE-TREATED SILL

GRAVEL

ANCHOR BOLT

REINFORCING BAR

CONCRETE

6"

6"

LOCAL CODE DEPTH

VAPOR BARRIER

REINFORCING BAR

4 Build the door framing by nailing pairs of studs to short lower plates and the full-length upper plate. Fasten the door framing in place with angled bridging studs as you did with the other wall sections. A dab of roofing cement or silicone sealant will help hold the lower plate in position on the slab.

5 A substantial header runs around the building to support the roof. To construct this header, fasten pairs of 6-foot-long 2-by-12 boards together, separated by 4-by-11¼-inch pieces of ½-inch exterior plywood. Place the plywood 2 inches from each end (to clear the miter cuts you will ultimately make) and on 2-foot centers in the middle; nail the plywood in place with 8d nails. Measure and cut each header section to be flush with the outer edge of the cap plate, and then miter the ends at 22½ degrees. Toenail the headers to the lower plates and to each other with 16d nails. Top the header with 2-by-4 upper plates, nailed in place.

6 To make the roof rafters, take a pair of 12-foot-long 2 by 8s and cut off one end of each at a 45-degree angle. Temporarily screw these cut ends to a scrap of 2 by 4 laid flat. Check that the rafters form a perfect 90-degree angle, and then add a temporary cross brace made of plywood

scrap about midway. With a helper, lift the assembly into position on the cap plate so the rafter ends bisect two opposite cap-plate corners. Next, center the assembly by measuring the overhang on each side, and then mark for the 1½-inch-deep bird's-mouth and 45-degree flush cuts at the tail of each rafter. Take the assembly down, make the cuts, lift it back up, and check the fit. Adjust as necessary. When you are satisfied with the fit, remove the assembly again and use the finished rafters to mark and cut six more.

7 With a table saw, rip the 4-foot-long 4-by-4 king post so that it has eight equal flats to accept the rafters and the rafter braces. Attach a pair of rafters to opposite sides of the king post with metal framing connectors and proprietary screws. Next, measure and cut two rafter cross braces, and attach them to the king post and to the rafters using some metal framing connectors and screws. Be sure the cross braces are level with each other and that they meet the king post at 90 degrees and the rafters at 45 degrees. Attach another set of rafters and braces to the king post, 90 degrees opposed to the first set. With helpers, lift this assembly into place and toenail it to the cap plate. Attach the remaining rafter pairs and cross braces to the king post and cap plate.

8 Cut and attach the 2-by-6 roof purlins, using metal joist hangers and proprietary screws. Measure, cut, and nail on ¾-inch plywood triangles atop the roof framing. If you intend to paint or stain the inner roof surface and framing, do so now. Add the clear acrylic-sheet section and its flashing, and seal it with silicone. With roofing nails, attach metal drip edging to the roof's perimeter. Shingle the roof. Bend and add hip shingles at the roof angles, and seal them with roofing cement. For the best appearance and weathertightness, top the roof with a metal cap (unless you are experienced in metalwork, you'll need to have this piece made). You can make up the cap from cut shingles and roofing cement, but this assembly may leak.

9 To cover the rough lumber and rafter ends, lending a finished appearance, first measure, cut, and add 1-by-12 and 1-by-6 horizontal trim boards to the roof header. Miter the corners at 22½ degrees, and nail on the trim with 8d finishing nails. With a table saw set at 22½ degrees, rip 1-by-4 (inside) and 1-by-6 (outside) vertical trim boards for each corner; crosscut them to fit, and nail them on with 8d finishing nails. Measure, cut, and nail jamb stock to the sides and top of the doorway, shimming as

needed to fit the doors. Cover the joint between the jambs and the framing with 1-by-4 and 1-by-6 ripped trim.

10 Paint or stain the structure and the doors as desired, and hang the doors. Next, pre-paint or stain the ⅜-by-1-inch screen-retainer stock. Staple screening in place over the openings, crosscut the screen retainers to fit, and nail them on with 4d galvanized finishing nails.

Framing Detail

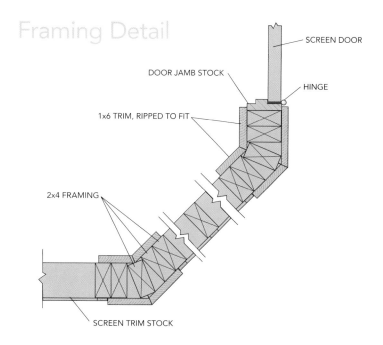

SCREEN DOOR

DOOR JAMB STOCK

HINGE

1x6 TRIM, RIPPED TO FIT

2x4 FRAMING

SCREEN TRIM STOCK

Choices of Screening Fabrics

Vinyl-coated fiberglass and aluminum are by far the most common screening fabrics used to enclose an outdoor structure. Of the two, vinyl-coated fiberglass is more popular because it is about half the price of aluminum. Solar, or "sun," screening is a tightly woven, energy-efficient variation of vinyl-coated fiberglass. It provides excellent shading and protects against heat gain.

The density of a screening's mesh determines its strength, the size of the bugs it will keep at bay, and the amount of light and breezes it will permit. If you want to stop tiny bugs such as no-see-ums, you can buy 20-by-20 mesh, but this will cut down on light transmission and breezes.

Metal screening is also available. Bronze screening is similar to aluminum but is far more expensive. Even more high-end are fabrics made from copper, brass, or stainless steel.

Specialty screenings include pet-resistant screen fabric made from heavy-duty, vinyl-coated polyester.

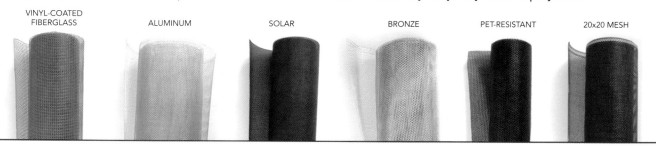

| VINYL-COATED FIBERGLASS | ALUMINUM | SOLAR | BRONZE | PET-RESISTANT | 20x20 MESH |

Credits

Photography

1 Robert Perron 2 Jerry Harpur 3 *top* Jessie Walker 3 *bottom* Diedra Walpole 5 Jean-Claude Hurni 6 Jay Graham 7 *top left* Christina Schmidhofer 7 *top right* Karen Bussolini 7 *bottom* Jean-Claude Hurni 8 *top left* Philip Harvey 8 *bottom right* Catriona Tudor Erler 9 *top* Jerry Harpur 9 *bottom* Van Chaplin 10 Van Chaplin 11 *top* Jessie Walker 11 *bottom right* Sylvia Martin/SPC Photo Collection 11 *bottom left* Saxon Holt 12 Jessie Walker 13 *top* Derek Fell 13 *bottom left* and *right* Jean-Claude Hurni 14 Michael Thompson 15 *top* E. Andrew McKinney 15 *bottom left* Michael S. Thompson 15 *bottom right* Derek Fell 16 Jean-Claude Hurni 17 *top left* Charles Mann 17 *top right* Peter O. Whitely 17 *bottom* Van Chaplin 18 *left* Lamontagne/The Garden Picture Library 18 *right* Jamie Hadley 19 *top* Jean-Claude Hurni 19 *bottom* Tim Street-Porter 20 Jamie Hadley 21 *top* Jamie Hadley 21 *bottom* Deidra Walpole 22 Tim Street-Porter 23 *top* Gay Bumgarner/Positive Images 23 *bottom* Meg McKinney Simle 24 *top left* Tim Street-Porter 24 *top right* Jean-Claude Hurni 24 *bottom* Jamie Hadley 25 Gay Bumgarner/Positive Images 26 *top left* Derek Fell 26 *top right* Jean-Claude Hurni 28 Van Chaplin 29 *top left* Jean-Claude Hurni 29 *top right* Jerry Harpur 29 *bottom* Stephen Cridland 30 *top* Saxon Holt 30 *bottom* Ian Adams 31 Tim Street-Porter 32 *top* Robert Perron 32 *bottom* Saxon Holt 33 *top* Saxon Holt 33 *middle* Derek Fell 33 *bottom* Michael S. Thompson 34 *top left* Derek Fell 34 *top right* Derek Fell 34 *bottom* Ken Gutmaker 35 Jean-Claude Hurni 36 Michael S. Thompson 37 *top* Marion Brenner 37 *bottom left* Derek Fell 37 *bottom right* Tim Street-Porter 38 *top* Jean-Claude Hurni 38 *bottom* Jessie Walker 39 SAE Builders 40 Derek Fell 41–42 *all* Vixen Hill Gazebos 43 Philip Harvey 44 *left* Summerwood Outdoors, Inc. 44 *top middle* and *top right* Vixen Hill Gazebos 44 *bottom right* David Baer 47 *top* Scott Fitzgerrell 48 Norman A. Plate 49 Philip Harvey 50–51 *all* HomeTips, Inc. 52 *measuring tape, combination square, hammer, plumb bob, level,* and *adjustable wrench* HomeTips, Inc. 52 *block plane, C-clamp, sliding bevel, crosscut saw, chisel,* and *miter box* Scott Fitzgerrell 52 *coping saw* Dan Stultz 53 *saber saw* and *circular saw* Dan Stultz 53 *drill* and *bits* Scott Fitzgerrell for HomeTips, Inc. 54 *reciprocating saw* Bosch Tools 54 *miter saw* and *router* Norman A. Plate 54 *safety equipment* Philip Harvey 55–57 *all* Norman A. Plate 60 *all* Dan Stultz 61 *all* Mark Rutherford 62 Frank Gaglione 63 Trowel Trades Red Lion 64–65 *all* Christopher Vendetta 66 David Baer, Smith-Baer Photography 67 *all* Christopher Vendetta 69–70 *all* HomeTips, Inc. 71–72 *all* Christopher Vendetta 73 *all* David Baer, Smith-Baer Photography 78 *top* Christopher Vendetta 78 *bottom* HomeTips, Inc. 79–80 *all* Christopher Vendetta 81 *all* B.C. Shake & Shingle Association 82–87 *all* Summerwood Outdoors, Inc. 88 Scott Atkinson 89–90 *all* Mark Rutherford 92–94 *all* David Baer, Smith-Baer Photography 95 *top right* David Baer, Smith-Baer Photography 95 *middle left* Tom Wyatt 96 Philip Harvey 100 Jamie Hadley 101–105 *all* Jean-Claude Hurni 106 Ken Chen 110 *top right* Steven Gunther 111–112 *all* Jamie Hadley 115 Jack McDowell 116 Sylvia Martin 119 Dennis Bettencourt 120 Philip Harvey 123 Tom Wyatt 124 Robert Perron 127–128 *all* Tom Wyatt 131 Jay Graham 132, 134 *all* Jean-Claude Hurni 136 Norman A. Plate 137 Tom Wyatt 138 Ernest Braun for the California Redwood Association 142–143 *all* Tom Wyatt 144 Courtesy of Pasadena Showcase House 2006 147 Tom Wyatt 148 Michael S. Thompson 151 Tom Wyatt 152 Saxon Holt 153 Sylvia Martin 157 *all* HomeTips, Inc.

Design

1 Design: Dan Haslegrave 6 Michael Glassman and Associates 7 *top right* Susan Muszulu 8 *top* Landscape Design: The Berger Partnership 11 *bottom right* Architects: Jane E. Treacy and Phillip R. Eagleburger, AIA/Treacy & Eagleburger Architects; Builder: Greg Davis/GPD Construction Co. 13 *bottom right* Design: Les Jardins d'Henriette (Henriette Miral) 16 Design: Ann Anderson 17 *top right* Design: Joleen & Tony Morales 18 *right* Architect: T. Scott Teas/TFH Architects 19 *top* Design: M-A. Fortier, Art & Jardins 19 *bottom* Design: Tichenor and Thorp 21 *top* Architectural and Interior Design: Pamela Dreyfuss Interior Design; Millwork and Doors: Creative Cabinets 21 *bottom* Design: New Leaf Garden Design 22 Design: Fung & Blatt Architects 23 *bottom* Architect: Patrick N. Fox 30 *top* Design: Jack Chandler 31 Design: Duccio Ermenegildo 33 *top* Design: Freeland Turner 34 *bottom* Architect/Builder: Bill Galli; Landscape Design: Peter Koenig 37 *top* Beni Strebel Tile 37 *bottom right* Design: Martha Stewart Living 39 Landscape Design: Michael Etchison 43 Van-Martin Rowe Design 95 *middle left* Landscape Architect: Rogers Gardens 96 Landscape Architect: R.M. Bradshaw & Associates 100 Design: Gazebo Nostalgia 101, 104 Design: Ginette Giugras 105 Architect: Jean-Claude Hurni 106 Design: David Snow, English Arbor Company 110 Architect: Robert C. Slenes and Morton Safford James III for Bennett, Johnson, Slenes & Smith 111, 112 Architect: Jared Polsky & Associates 115 Landscape Architect: The Peridian Group 116 Landscape Architect: J. Starbuck 119 Architect: Hooper, Olmstead and Hrovat for the California Redwood Association; Landscape Architect: Casey A. Kawamoto 120 Landscape Architect: Lankford Associates 123 Landscape Architect: Forsum/Summers & Partners 124 Design: Dan Haslegrave 127 Landscape Architect: John J. Greenwood & Associates, Inc. 128 Design: Mark Hajjar 131 Design/Builder: Peter O. Whitely 132–134 Architect: Jean-Claude Hurni 136 Architect: Thomas Higley 137 Landscape Architect: Forsum/Summers & Partners 138 Design/Builder: Henry Angeli 142 Landscape Architect: Forsum/Summers & Partners 143 Landscape Architect: Forsum/Summers & Partners 144 Design: C & K Landscape Design for the Pasadena Showcase House 2006 147 Landscape Architect: Forsum/Summers & Partners 148 Design: Elizabeth Lair 151 Design: Philip Neumann 153 Architect: Lou Kimball, AIA

Resources

Alumawood
(888) ALUMAWOOD
www.alumawood.com

APA—The Engineered Wood Association
(253) 565-6600
www.apawood.org

American Society of Landscape Architects
(202) 898-2444
www.asla.org

American Wood Council
(202) 463-2766
www.awc.org

B.C. Shake & Shingle Association
(604) 820-7700
www.cedarbureau.org

Bella Vista Gazebos
(800) 600-0299
www.4gazebos.com

California Redwood Association
(800) 225-7339
www.calredwood.org

Dalton Pavilions, Inc.
(800) 532-5866
www.daltonpavilions.com

Pacific Columns
(800) 294-1098
www.pacificcolumns.com

Summerwood Outdoors, Inc.
(866) 519-4634
www.summerwood.com

Vixen Hill Gazebos
(610) 286-0909
www.vixenhill.com

Index

A

Acrylic plastic, 35–36, 152–157
Aluminum, 38–39, 157
Anatomy of structures, 44–45
Anchor bolts, 50–51, 60–61, 66
Arbors, 10–11, 14–17, 106–109, 111–115, 131, 138–141, 148–152
Architects, 40–41
Awnings, 36–38
Asphalt shingles, 33, 35, 78–80

B

Bamboo, 31
Base maps, 27
Battens, 29, 76–77
Batterboards, 62–63, 65
Beams, 45–46, 48–49, 61, 68–72, 94, 98. *See also Rafters*
Bean poles, 31
Benches, 128–131
Bids, construction, 41–42
Blocking, for rafters, 73, 86
Board feet, 47
Boards, 29, 74–77
Bolts, 50–51, 57
Bower, garden, 148–151
Bracing, for rafters, 73
Budgets, 43
Builders, 40–41
Building
    codes and permits, 27, 48, 65, 89
    designers, 40–41
    materials (*See Materials*)
    methods, 44–91

C

Canvas, 36–38
Ceiling fans, 91
Codes and permits, 27, 48, 65, 89
Columns, 32–33, 46, 68, 85, 111–114, 123–127, 144–147.
    See also Posts
Concrete, 45–46, 60–61, 63, 66–67, 154–156. *See also Footings*

Contractors and contracts, 40–42
Copper roofing, 34
Cotton duck, 36–38
Cutting
    beams and rafters, 72, 93, 99, 104
    posts, 70
    shingles, 80, 81
    tools, 52–57
    underlayment, 79
    wood, 55–57

D

Decks, building on, 46, 61, 96–99, 101–105, 116–118, 124–130, 132–136, 138–141
Design 7, 25–27, 40–41
Draftspersons, 41
Drilling, 53, 57, 60, 65, 93
Drip edge flashing, 79
Drywall screws, 50

E

Easements, 27
Egg crate roofing, 75
Electrical, 41, 89–91
Engineers, 41
Entryways, 10–11, 14–15
Expanding anchor bolts, 50–51, 60

F

Fabric roofing, 36–38
Fascia, 78
Fasteners, 50–51, 57, 59–60
Felt, roofing, 78–80
Fiberglass
    columns, 32, 111–114, 124–127, 144–147
    roofing, 36
    screening, 38–39, 157
Finishing wood, 68, 88
Flashing, 58–59, 79–80
Floors, gazebo, 61, 84–85, 98
Footings, 60–66, 83–84, 93–94, 97–98, 102–103, 105, 107–108,

112–114, 117–118, 121–122, 125–126, 133–135, 139–141, 146
Foundations, 41, 45–46, 60–67, 83–84, 156. *See also Footings*
Framing connectors, 51, 61, 70–71, 84

G

Garden rooms, 18–19, 23, 116–119, 136, 153–157
Gazebo
    hubs, 42, 45, 87, 97–99
    kits, 13, 43, 82–87, 100
Gazebos, 5, 12–13, 18, 33–35, 40, 44–45, 74, 82–87, 96–99, 100, 128–131, 132–133, 136, 153–157
General contractors, 40–41
GFCI receptacles, 89–90
Glass roofing, 35–36
Grape stakes, 31

H

Hip and ridge shingles, 79–80
House-attached overheads, 58–59, 62–63, 72, 101–104, 111–118, 124–127, 138–143
Hubs, gazebo, 42, 45, 87, 97–99
Hurricane anchors, 51, 72–73

I

Insects, screening for, 38–39, 157

J

Joinery, 56–57
Joist hangers, 51, 58, 61
Joists, on piers, 61, 84

K

Kit gazebos, 13, 43, 82–87, 100

L

Lag screws, 50–51, 57–58, 60
Landscape professionals, 40–41
Lath, 29, 75–77
Lattice, 29, 32, 75, 101–105, 115, 128–131, 137, 143, 151

Ledgers, 46, 58–59, 62, 71–72, 101–104, 125–127, 138–141
Legal restrictions, 27
Lighting, 89–91
Lodge poles, 31
Louvered roofing, 77
Lumber, buying, 47–49

M

Manufactured structures, 13, 39, 43, 82–87, 100
Masonry
  anchors, 50–51, 60–61
  contractors, 41
Materials
  budgeting for, 43
  buying, 47–51
  selecting, 28–39
  specifying in contracts, 42
Microclimates, 26–27,
Miters, 53–54, 56, 95

N

Nails, 50

O

Open sheathing, 74
Outlets, electrical, 89–91

P

Painting, 68, 88
Patio, building on, 60–61
Pergolas, 8–10
Permits, 27, 65
Piers (*See Footings*)
Pilot holes, 57
Planning, 22–43
Plastic
  screening, 39, 157
  roofing, 35–36, 75
Plumbing contractors, 41
Plywood, 30–31
  roofing, 34
  sheathing, 74, 78–80
Poles, 31
Pool shelter, 101–105

Porch screening, 39, 157
Posts
  anchoring, 61, 66, 93
  bases and anchors for, 51, 69, 97
  caps for, 51, 73
  detailing, 95
  erecting, 93–94
  gazebo, 84–85, 98–99
  installing, 68–71
  types of, 32
Preservative-treated lumber, 47, 49, 69
Professionals, 40–41

R

Rafters, 45–46, 48–49, 51, 59, 68, 71–74, 76–77, 86–87, 94–95, 99, 104. *See also Beams*
Rafter spans, 48–49
Railings, 99
Rain and snow, 26
Receptacles, electrical, 89–91
Roof pitch, 78
Roof sections, gazebo, 87
Roofing, 7, 74–81
  asphalt shingles, 33, 35, 78–80
  attaching to house, 7
  fabric, 36–38
  felt, 78–80
  for gazebos, 86–89
  louvered, 77
  open, 74–77
  plastic and glass, 35–36, 75
  solid, 33–35, 74, 78–81

S

Safety, 54
Saws, 52–56, 70
Schedules, in contracts, 42
Screening, 38–39, 157
Screws, 50
Seismic anchors, 51, 73
Shade cloth, 75
Sheathing, 74, 78–80
Shingles, 33, 35, 78–81
Siding, cutting house, 58
Site selection, 25–26, 62–63

Slabs, 45–46, 60–61, 66–67. *See also Concrete*
Soils engineers, 41
Spa shelter, 101–104
Spans, 48–49, 76
Staining, 68, 88
Steel, 30, 32, 33, 39
Structural engineers, 41
Stucco columns, 33, 123, 147
Subcontractors, 41
Sun exposure, 23, 26, 39
Switches, electrical, 90

T

Tea arbor, 106–109
Tile roofing, 34–35
Tools, 52–57
Treated lumber, 47, 49, 69
Trellises, 111–115, 120–123, 138–141
Trim, for posts, 73, 95

U

Underlayment, roof, 78–80
UV blockers, 88

V

Vegas, 31
Vines, 112, 152
Vinyl components, 32, 36, 83

W

Window screening, 38–39
Wiring, 89–91
Wood
  basics, 28–29, 47–49
  products, 31–32
  shingles, 33, 81
  sidings, 33–35
Woven bamboo and reed, 31, 75

Y

Y bracing, for posts, 71

Z

Z flashing, 59
Zoning ordinances, 27